THE

AMOROUS

COSMOS

THE AMOROUS COSMOS: WELCOME HOME SIGNS IN REALITY

FROM PRE-TRAGIC TO TRAGIC TO POST-TRAGIC

• • •

First Principles and First Values in Response to the Meta-Crisis

Eros Mystery Schools: Oral Essays, Vol. 3

DR. MARC GAFNI

Author: Gafni, Marc
Title: The Amorous Cosmos
Identifiers: ISBN 979-8-88834-009-7 (electronic)
ISBN 979-8–88834–008–0 (paperback)

© 2024 Marc Gafni

Cover photo: "Caldwell 69"
Credit: NASA/Goddard/Arizona State University

Edited by Kathy Brownback, Krista Josepha, and Jeffrey Malecki

World Philosophy and Religion Press,
in conjunction with

IP Integral Publishers

https://worldphilosophyandreligion.org

We are in a time between stories, a time between worlds, poised between utopia and dystopia, facing unprecedented existential risks that threaten humanity. Only a new Story of shared global value will allow us to respond effectively to our shared global challenges and turn our potentially dire fate into a new collective date with destiny. The old stories no longer hold, and many of us no longer even believe in the possibility of story, or value—or a Story of Value. The natural impulse in face of the unbearable tragic is often to turn away, to revert to the "pre-tragic." We've been doing this—individually and collectively—for far too long. We must now, with the trembling joy of responsibility, turn towards the tragic, feeling all that comes up, in order to haltingly and courageously find our way toward a post-tragic consciousness. We begin in the realization that we're always already truly welcome in the Amorous Cosmos. From that consciousness we then place our attention on the articulation of a new Story of Value as the only response to the meta-crisis. Only from the post-tragic can we recover a "memory of the future," a non-naïve hope, as we realize the New Human and the New Humanity, *Homo amor*, who recognizes value "anthro-ontologically"—from within. From this place can we see the gorgeous potential of living lives of Outrageous Love, gathered into "Unique Self Symphonies" that serve all beings—and that serve the whole of Reality itself. In this we become partners with the Divine—with God—whom we call the "Infinite Intimate." We are unique incarnations of the Infinite Intimate. The awakening to this precise realization is the crossing over from Homo sapiens to *Homo amor*.

This volume features a series of connected "oral essays," texts that express the Dharma that was delivered at the annual week-long Eros Mystery School, by Dr. Marc Gafni. They have been edited specifically to be read and absorbed, so that the Dharma is transmitted directly. They also include analyses of cultural texts (popular movies and songs) that represent crucial— and often hidden or unconscious—aspects of the emergent New Story of Value. This volume features frequent recapitulations of key themes, which both review previous material and add new emphases and perspectives. In addition, the various prayers, meditations, and contemplation practices are designed to give you an embodied, anthro-ontological sense of the unimaginably beautiful transformations, both personal and collective, that are not only possible but absolutely necessary for responding to the meta-crisis and existential risk.

These oral essays are edited talks delivered by Marc
Gafni at the Eros Mystery School, August 2021.

erosmysteryschool.com

CONTENTS

CHAPTER 2: FROM TRAGIC TO POST-TRAGIC—A VIEW OF WHAT IS POSSIBLE: THE VISION OF HOPE AND POSSIBILITY, AND WHY THE DOOMERS ARE WRONG

CHAPTER 3: ARE WE WELCOME IN COSMOS? THE MOTHER AND THE BIRTH OF HOMO AMOR IN EARLY BIBLICAL CONSCIOUSNESS

CHAPTER 4: THE DANCE BETWEEN CERTAINTY AND UNCERTAINTY

CHAPTER 5: FIRST PRINCIPLES & FIRST VALUES

INTRODUCTION

by Claire Molinard

It's an honor and a privilege to introduce you to someone who needs no introduction. Dr. Marc Gafni, as many of you here know, has dedicated his whole life's work to what he calls the Evolution of Love. With his unique combination of brilliant mind and passion, plus the depth and poignancy of his heart, Marc is articulating a vision for what is possible for humanity today—a vision grounded in the integrated insights of the leading edges of traditional, modern, and postmodern wisdom streams.

He weaves this vision together like a magician, and that vision has become what we call the Dharma, which is an ever-evolving tapestry. We are proud to be a container for this unfolding Dharma. In this time between worlds, in this time between stories, it's more urgent than ever that we are allured to the new Universe Story that Marc is articulating.

That's why we're here together. That's why we have been drawn to creating this new Universe Story, a story of Outrageous Love that can literally pave the way for a Planetary Awakening in Love through Unique Self Symphonies, which is what we really are.

We are allured to a story that calls each person to rise up to his or her greatness and to move from a global success story of zero-sum rivalrous dynamics to a story in which everyone has their part in co-creating and co-evolving for *the Good, the True, and the Beautiful.*

CHAPTER 1

SENSING INTO EXISTENTIAL RISK

FROM THE PRE-TRAGIC TO THE TRAGIC

1.1

POISED BETWEEN UTOPIA AND DYSTOPIA: TAKING DYSTOPIA SERIOUSLY

It's a big moment in time, a big moment in history. What I'd like to do is something actually quite difficult, so I want to find our way in gently, slowly, gradually. And with your permission, I'm first going to *complexify* the space before things get more clear. We're aiming for "second simplicity," as we call it—the simplicity that comes after acknowledging all the complexity.

We often say that **we're in this moment between utopia and dystopia**, and in some sense, it's really hard to get what that sentence means. In order to chart a path to a world in which literally billions of people *don't* die—which is, as we'll see, a possibility on the current trajectory, on many levels—we have to actually find our way inside and through.

We actually have the capacity together to move one major step forward, based precisely on the people gathered at the Mystery School, online around the world, as well as anyone listening to or reading this book. In fact, if you're now listening to or reading the book, *you specifically, this precise group of people,* can actually come together and articulate a re-

sponse to the potential dystopia in a way that no other group of people in the world can do quite like we can.

Not that we're better than anyone else in the world—that would be absurd—but rather that we all have a particular instrument to play in what we call the Unique Self Symphony.

THE JOYFUL PATH OUT OF DYSTOPIA AND DESTRUCTION

I want to honor everyone who's listening to or reading this—there will be many who are new to this Dharma. I want to honor everyone. I don't want to take you into a field of discourse where there's an implicit meaning to many words you may not know.

What we call Unique Self Symphony is very different from the pseudo-harmonies of the hive mind being generated in the digital world, which are leading to various forms of digital dictatorship. It's also very different from a reductive materialist view. Unique Self Symphony itself is an emergent property of evolutionary intimacy among Unique Selves. And by Unique Self, we don't mean separate self, the person with their particular Myers-Briggs test results. **By Unique Self, we mean: every unique incarnation of the Infinite Personhood of Cosmos, with its irreducibly unique qualities of being and becoming—and an irreducibly unique quality of intimacy.**

Each Unique Self has particular gifts to give that are needed by the whole. Every one of those Unique Selves can play their unique instrument, which, when played together, become part of the Unique Self Symphony. That vision by itself is a vision of Value, which, were it to be adopted, has massively beneficial implications in:

- ◆ Educational policy
- ◆ Social policy
- ◆ Economic policy

- ◆ Politics
- ◆ Governance

To take seriously this vision of Unique Self and the vision of Unique Self Symphony would change the direction of Reality.

So many view the statement that we are poised between utopia and dystopia without due seriousness, as though the work we are doing to enact this new narrative of identity were a hobby or spiritual pastime. We spend a bit of time on it because it's supposedly good for us, but we don't actually take it seriously. **We don't get what it means to say: we're literally poised between utopia and dystopia.**

It's an incredible sentence.

In 2013 or so, I asked everyone to read a book by Ramez Naam, *The Infinite Resource*. It's the single best book on this topic. This book is profoundly flawed, but at least it lays out the great challenges of what it would mean to actually slide into dystopia. We don't get what dystopia means because it's so difficult to take dystopia truly seriously.

Robert Jay Lifton, a sociologist and psychologist from within the mainstream academy, is one of the first people who fully understood the implications of the current apocalypse. In the 1970s, he wrote about brainwashing, Chinese concentration camps, and Nazi doctors. In his contribution to a powerful book from the 1980s called *Facing Apocalypse*, he claims **the reason we don't take seriously the potential of apocalypse, of dystopia, is because it is unimaginable.** How do we imagine the unimaginable? How do we actually feel into it?

In order to imagine it in any way, we cannot use only the Eye of the Mind—with its rational discourse, statistics, analyses, and facts. Nor can we grasp it only empirically, with the Eye of the Senses. We need the third eye, the Eye of the Heart—we need to feel it in our bodies.

Just like in good mysticism, we're trying, through meditation, or prayer, or contemplation, to non-conceptually access the ground of consciousness that's our deepest identity, which we often call True Self. **To truly begin to understand apocalypse/dystopia, we must access it in a non-conceptual way.**

• • •

Very gently now, try to access—in your heart, your body, and your mind— the potential reality that by the year 2040, of the nearly eight billion people currently on the planet, the majority are dead. Let's see if we can access that reality, and then make it personal, to get a non-conceptual sense in our heart, body, and mind. Imagine that you're out of food and that you won't last more than a week. We have the capacity to enter deeply into this reality.

What we're suggesting is that, with the resources we have in this Unique Self Symphony, we *can* change this trajectory—we're just not yet activated. We're not even near maximal capacity for effective action.

We cannot activate from a place of fear, trepidation, or anxiety, but only with an enormous sense of joy, a feeling of unimaginable purpose, un-imaginable Outrageous Love, unimaginable passion, and even delight in this very moment. The path out of dystopia is motivated not only by the urgency of fear, but by the ecstatic urgency of love and possibility.

1.2

THE DESTRUCTION OF THE TEMPLE IN JERUSALEM

There's a beautiful text in the interior sciences, a complete esoteric tradition that talks about the destruction of the temple in Jerusalem. The temple was originally built by Solomon in Ancient Jerusalem, and was destroyed four hundred years later. It was rebuilt by Ezra with the facilitation of Darius, the King of Persia. When that second temple was destroyed five hundred years later, a description of this event was transmitted in a document over several hundred years.

The original tradition, expressed in the Mary Magdalene tradition in Christianity, is sourced in the temple tradition—which is the source of Greek Hermeticism, and the source of most modern science from Jerusalem via Alexandria in the first century, and then into Hellenism, ultimately seeding the best of the Western tradition.

This original temple tradition in Jerusalem has an ark at its center, called the Ark of the Covenant. Based on a close philological reading of the Hebrew sources and the interior science traditions, we know that **above the Ark there were two cherubs, passionately, erotically entwined and filled with Outrageous Love.** There is a tradition that says, at a time in which the community is aligned with the value of Cosmos, the cherubs are face-to-face in Outrageous Love and passionate embrace. But this is a time when the community is not aligned, the community is somehow alienated from *ratzon*, from the will of Cosmos that lives in us and flows through us. At this time, the cherubs are not face-to-face, but back-to-back. They lose that sense of Outrageous Love, they lose their aliveness, they lose their passion.

However, in the third century, the Talmud speaks of *a time when the destruction of home is imminent.* The esoteric priests who witness what happens in the Holy of Holies said that at that time of imminent destruction, at that time of proto-risk, the cherubs were actually in passionate embrace.

They were filled with *Eros.*

They were filled with aliveness.

They were radically alive.

We're at that moment now.

1.3

RESPONDING TO EXISTENTIAL RISK AS *HOMO AMOR*, THE FULFILLMENT OF *HOMO SAPIENS*

We are poised between utopia and dystopia, but what does it really mean, in Robert Jay Lifton's words, to face apocalypse, to face the unimaginable? That's part of what it means to be a human being at this moment in time. The human being is Adam, which includes both Eve and Adam. The original Adam is minimally transgender—and includes all the masculine and the feminine, and all the shades and permutations in between. The original **word *adam*, human, means both ground and imagination**.

The human being is Homo imaginus.

To be *Homo imaginus* at this time, to ground the electricity of existential risk and to be able to respond to it, we first need to be able to face it. We can step closer, we can step back, but we can never look away—that's the demand of Eros. **One of the core qualities of the New Human and the New Humanity**—which we call *Homo amor*, who has the capacity to respond to catastrophic and existential risk and transform Reality—**is a deeply evolved understanding of what it means to be certain, and what uncertainty is.** *Homo amor* **incarnates both certainty and uncertainty.**

They say that the voice of God emerges from the space between the cherubs above the Ark of the Covenant. All of us are the cherubs, so let us be passionately embraced in Outrageous Love. From the space between us will emerge a new voice, a new resource, a new possibility. *And if God is anything, then God is the Possibility of Possibility.*

We are in this time between worlds. We are facing not just one pandemic called Covid, but potentially multiple pandemics over the next decade—and that's just the beginning of a much longer, more complex story. **The only way to respond to existential risk is to articulate a new global story—not a fanciful story, not a conjecture, not a best-seller, but a Great Library that tells us something about who we are as human beings, bringing together new sets of facts across entire disciplines, and aggregating and** *integrating new configurations of intimacy:*

- A new narrative of identity.
- A new narrative of community.
- A new narrative of power.
- A new narrative of desire.
- A new universe story.

If we want to address this yawning chasm and imagine the unimaginable, we must generate a new source code so self-evident that it will be adopted long after we're all gone and forgotten. And it can't be written by one person—**it must emerge from the community, from our sense of loving each other. It must emerge from the space between the cherubs—and we are the cherubs.**

That's what changes the world we live in. That's what da Vinci understood in the Renaissance—in a time between worlds and time between stories. As Paul Tillich points out, there were no more than a thousand people involved at the core of the Renaissance. Da Vinci and his cohort told a New

Story based on the integration of all the best facts of interior and exterior science available at the time, integrated into a new whole greater than the sum of the parts *so compelling* it changed the trajectory of Reality.

We too must tell a compelling New Story of Value filled with *telos* and Eros, aligned with the deepest reading of the sciences in both interior and exterior that evokes the fulfillment of *Homo sapiens* into *Homo amor*, and transmits an actual vision of the amorous Cosmos. It's the only thing that's going to change the trajectory of everything, the way da Vinci, Marsilio Ficino, along with three or four dozen other people, completely changed the trajectory of human history by helping to usher in modernity—not because they went into every village and healed the Black Death, but because they told a story which involved a new way of thinking, a new way of feeling, and a new way of being.

They ushered in a New Human and a New Humanity that changed the source code of reality itself.

The response we're developing here will help to change everything—and nothing else will.

1.4

THREE LEVELS OF CONSCIOUSNESS: PRE-TRAGIC, TRAGIC, POST-TRAGIC

To develop our capacity to enact that response, we must go through three stages. The first stage is recognizing that even though we're one of the few hubs in the world that's been talking about this in a serious way, even we are still pre-tragic in some ways. So before we get to radical hope, I want to actually chart this path together with you from the pre-tragic to the tragic to the post-tragic. These are three levels of consciousness.

What does the pre-tragic mean? The pre-tragic means that I haven't fully faced the tragedy.

There's a powerful moment in Kathy Brownback's wonderful book about transmitting the core structures of the New Story, particularly the story of Unique Self to the world of secondary school education, where she talks about the deepening awareness of tragedy when her husband was going through a very challenging time. This is what we mean by moving beyond the pre-tragic. You move beyond the pre-tragic either because you or someone you know face an impending illness or death. Your world falls apart.

You get fired, or a marriage you thought was going to last forever doesn't, or you experience a betrayal, or come up against the edge of a limitation, or recognize something about yourself and your shadow. "I didn't know I was capable of this or that." In other words, you face up to some limitation of yourself. **You move out of the pre-tragic as a way of making sense of the world.**

My beautiful brother David, who passed away five years ago in a car crash, was a gorgeous expression of ethnocentric fundamentalism. At his funeral there were thousands of people. He had no resources, no organization, no finances. His wife, Miriam, was my assistant for a bunch of years when I was running a teaching organization in New York City's public schools and private schools. From their perspective, they took over my outreach work in the Jewish community, focused on inviting Jews to return to orthodoxy, which is what I spent a couple years of my life doing. David was and is in his next stage of the journey. They lived in Staten Island, and anyone who needed anything would come to their house for anything, day or night.

Whenever something would go wrong in the world, I'd speak to David, and he would immediately "know" why it happened. He would explain, citing some text, that this was God's purpose. He had all the available tools of classical religion. He lived in the pre-tragic because, no matter what happened, even the Holocaust, he had a set of tools that explained it. **That's the pre-tragic mode of consciousness: You experience some tragedy, but you've immediately got it all figured out.**

You've got a radical certainty, an inappropriate certainty, a certainty that violates Spirit. You're absolutely certain your model is the *only* model. But whether it's a scientific or a religious model, the model is never the Reality. The map is not the territory, and the belief in the model comes between my direct experience of Reality, violating my radical empiricism, my own internal knowing. From this perspective, the Eye of the Senses rigidifies my senses, the Eye of the Heart closes my heart, and the Eye of the Mind distorts and even corrupts my mind. The pre-tragic corrupts these three great eyes of perception.

At their best:

- The Eye of the Senses includes empirical ways of knowing.
- The Eye of Heart opens me to the wider field of Eros, passion, and kindness.
- The Eye of the Mind includes logic, mathematics, reasoning.

But they all become distorted when you have a dogmatic model that comes between you and the three eyes, each with their own unique capacity to perceive Reality.

Pre-tragic means: I haven't confronted the fullness of the tragedy. I haven't been willing to sit in it. I'm somehow looking away.

Then there often comes a certain moment when I can't look away anymore. I collapse. *I've got to stop, look, and step in to find radiance.* **At this moment, I embrace the tragic unflinchingly, with full grief, with full broken heart—this is the only way I can move from the pre-tragic to the tragic.** Only after I've fully embraced the tragic can I then go to the post-tragic. Without doing this, words like utopia and dystopia literally become just part of our mental furniture. We don't actually know what they mean. We have to face the tragic in a deep and real way.

That's what Yeats meant in his "Dialogue of Self and Soul": *When such as I cast out remorse*—when such as I have moved to the tragic—when I haven't avoided it, I've let go of all my explanatory models, I've faced my shadow and walked through it, I've owned the darkest possibility of Self and the larger Reality, only then I can say:

> *When such as I cast out remorse,*
> *So great a sweetness fills my breast.*
> *We must laugh, and we must sing.*
> *We are blest by everything,*
> *Everything we look upon is blest.*

That's the frame through which we embrace the full tragedy.

CONTEMPLATIVE EXERCISE: JOURNALING ON THE PRE-TRAGIC, TRAGIC, AND POST-TRAGIC

We're about to walk into the tragic, then we're going to walk through it to the post-tragic. To get to the post-tragic we're going to need a new story. We need to articulate this new story in a new way together—we're going to need to deliver it into Reality to deliver Homo amor, this new vision of the New Human and New Humanity, into Reality together. But we're not going to get there yet.

Take ten or twenty minutes and journal about what we've talked about so far. Really stay focused on this movement from pre-tragic, to tragic, to post-tragic, to prepare ourselves to face Reality in a new way.

From your particular, personal perspective, what are the massive changes that we're going through at the moment?

What are the ways you may be naively staying in the pre-tragic?

How can you move beyond? Are there ways that you have been stuck in the tragic before? Are there specific blocks that you know of that may prevent you from moving to the post-tragic?

Notice if you start to avoid an engagement with these difficult issues. See if you can refrain from the deflection. Be gentle, but see if you can stay with it.

1.5

FACING INTO THE TRAGIC: THE DEATH OF OUR HUMANITY

I'm going to try and take you into conversations that are taking place behind the scenes today. I'm going to read you some unpublished conversations. We're going to take some surprising turns—we've never directly faced the tragic in this particular way.

Directly facing the tragic is the beginning of the unveiling, the meaning of the Greek word *apocalypse*—the revealing. In Hebrew, "world" is *olam*, which means "the place of hiddenness." When we move to the apocalypse, it challenges the hiddenness. We intuit that *there's something that wants to be disclosed*. But in order to get to that which wants to be disclosed, the new emergence, the new joy, in order to get from *Homo sapiens* to *Homo amor*, we must face the tragic. **We can't just jump from the pre-tragic to the post-tragic—we can't only laugh and sing in order to generate a New Human and a New Humanity. We can't flip the switch from dystopia to utopia.**

We can't bypass the tragic.

If we don't want to see the tragic realized, through actual fulfillment of existential risk—and a number of very plausible scenarios forecast the death of most, if not all, human beings on the planet—**if we don't want to go down that road, then we must face the tragic by fully *imagining* it, *feeling* it, and *seeing* it clearly.**

When we talk about existential risk, we're always talking about two kinds: The first we call the death of humanity, and the second we call the death of *our* humanity. The first is the physical death of the entire human species—everyone. The second is just as bad, if not worse: the death of what we recognize to be a human being, with its salient characteristics—joy, love, freedom, free will, the drama of decision-making, and human dignity.

Homo amor, the New Human, following the story based on evolving First Values and First Principles, must be able to respond to both kinds of existential risk.

1.6

EMBRACING THE TRAGIC: EVOLUTIONARY THOUGHT, POST-DOOM AND BEYOND

I will share two scenarios illustrating the embracing of the tragic. The first is from an unpublished transcript of a conversation between two friends of mine, both significant figures and colleagues and—like myself—deeply involved in what we might call "evolutionary thinking and teaching." One I'm going to call Jack, and the other I'm going to call Tom (names changed to protect the innocent).

Jack is still very classically evolutionary, while Tom has abandoned the evolutionary position and views himself as a "post-Doomer." His basic point, along with quite a few of the smartest people in the world today, is that people are refusing to face what's coming. He is basing his view on a decade of serious research into intense, cascading levels of facts, a profound examination of the "planetary stack," as Benjamin Bratton calls it: the economic structure, the physical structure, the mineral structure, the governance structures, the social structures, the technological structures, and the causal factors that destabilize them.

Here's the transcript of that conversation:

Tom: "It was around December 2012 when I had my sort of climate come-to-Jesus moment—that's when I really turned my back on what had been my primary worldview and orientation from 2000 to December of 2012. My book, which became one of the major books in the world on this, expressed my original view that I then turned my back on."

Jack: "Yeah, I remember your book. It was super inspiring."

Tom: "When I got climate change for real and then started to get what abrupt climate change might mean for us, what happened is most of the people, for example, in the integral community that I was related to, at least in part, the people that surround you and your friends and the people around our friend, Ken— they stopped inviting me to speak. They thought this was a little too Doomsday for them. They didn't want to look at it. At some point, I read something by Paul Kingsnorth and Dougald Hine called the *Dark Mountain Manifesto*."

The *Dark Mountain Manifesto* is the apocalypse manifesto of serious thinkers who say we have to face the tragic.

Tom: "I thought it was kick-ass, so I sent it to one of our friends, one of the key figures, and he said he wasn't interested in this kind of thing. He just didn't want to talk to me about it, period. But then I sent it to 'Rick' and his response was just incredibly clear and upfront. He said, 'Tom, I find this *Dark Mountain Manifesto* to be philosophically incoherent, morally repulsive, and morally repugnant. Please never share anything like this with me again.' That was the response I got."

Jack: "I was in Boulder and I spent three days with a close former student of mine and I then tried to share some of this with him, and he said 'this is ridiculous.' Now, five years later, everyone is saying, 'Holy shit, what the fuck is happening?' Maybe it's not ridiculous."

Tom: "Exactly. That's one of the reasons why, in my latest videos, I make sure that I let people know that denial has a bad rap. We have good instincts for denial, for some really good reasons. There's people who deny in order to be able to wake up every day and be present to their kids, their job, their grandkids. They don't want to hang out in Doomland. I get it. But in the end, denial doesn't work."

Jack: "Well, I'm curious, how do you hold the large scale of it all now? How do you hold the sense that things are progressing?"

Tom: "One of the most difficult things for people to let go of is the myth of perpetual progress. Shifting from that progressive worldview—spiritually progressive, technologically optimistic, and socially conscious—to the very real possibility of extinction in the not-too-distant future, and certainly to the collapse of industrial humanity… that's hard for people to do. People are generally not willing to do this."

Jack: "Here's the question I want to ask you. I get that things are as bad and maybe even worse than they appear, and tragically, we're not rising to the occasion. I get that the smartest people are all catching on to this, but I still feel connected to the evolutionary impulse. How do you put these things together?"

Tom: "One of the big shifts that's happened to me, is that in the first stage when I wrote my big book on evolution, evolution was the foreground; it was at the center and ecology was in the background—now that's shifted for me. Ecology is now fundamental. For example, when I read John Stewart's book *Evolution's Arrow*, I was evangelistic about that for many years. Now I think it's just completely deluded. I don't dismiss the whole book. Some of it's still brilliant, but the basic notion of never-ending complexification and cooperation at larger and wider scale—I can't hold that anymore. I now understand the

19

beginning of the rise and fall of civilizations. I didn't understand back then the difference between a genuinely sustainable culture that preserves the biosphere and basically treats it as if it's a Divine Being, and cultures of extraction that are all about manipulating the biosphere for human benefit and measure wealth and human well-being in only human-centered terms, not in life-centered terms. That's been one of the big developments in my own education."

Jack: "What about hope?"

Tom: "I find this quote from Stephen Jenkinson to be quite helpful."

Stephen Jenkinson is another prominent figure in the post-Doomer community.

Tom: "Jenkinson says, 'Grief work requires us to know the time we're in. The great enemy of grief is hope. Hope is the four-letter word for people who are unwilling to know things for what they are. Our time requires us to be hope-free, to burn through the false choices of being hopeful or hopeless. These are two sides of the same con job. Grief is required to proceed. So I pretty much hang out in a hope-free space. I'm joyous, I love life, I'm present. But I'm in a hope-free space."

Jack: "So in terms of the points you've made about evolution being a movement of constant progress and complexification, can you still hold that to be true in the big picture?"

Tom: "No, I don't even hold that anymore. I don't hold evolution as a process. I don't hold evolution to be a process of getting bigger, better, or more conscious. I used to, and in fact the first chapter of my book talks about that, but I don't sell my book anymore because although I agree with ninety percent of it, there's that ten percent I completely don't agree with. I don't agree with the belief in progress anymore. I don't believe in holding progress as a secular faith or a secular religion or whatever. I lean towards this sense that everything that modernity has accomplished has been a product of modernist arrogance, and that our 'great' accomplishments have been largely ecocidal. The advancement of humankind and the advancement of technology and consciousness have all been framed in anthropocentric terms, but actually we've got to move from the anthropocentric to the biocentric, and say that progress that is only anthropocentric violates Reality."

Jack: "Yeah, this should be the challenge, right?"

Tom: "Yeah, if any human being survives this bottleneck, it's a big deal. Sure, there's been tremendous benefit and ease and wealth and longevity. All the good stuff that Stephen Pinker and his friends point to. But if you don't have an ecological paradigm, if you haven't read, for example, Catton's 1980 *Overshoot*, then you don't get the fundamental ecological view. I think *Overshoot* was the most important book I ever read. All the things that Stephen Pinker counts—he's got dozens and dozens of charts, but every one of them goes down if you understand *Overshoot*. Every single natural system, without exception, that we depend on is not just in decline, but in precipitous freefall. For years, I'd read John Stewart, I read Ken Wilber, I trained with Don Beck, and I tried to put together the *techozoic*"—meaning technology with ecology—"and I heard, after he died, that Thomas Berry had lost faith in me because he saw me trying to do this integration, and he thought I was wrong. Now I realize that I *was* wrong."

Jack: "What do you think is going to happen?"

Tom: "Even if industrial civilization were to collapse, or just as significantly, even with a twenty or thirty percent shift away from fossil-fuel burning, the earth would still heat up another degree within a matter of a few months. It's the real reason why I don't have hope. I think we're already in a runaway mode. I think that every year from now on, the major forests of the world, including the Amazon and the boreal forests of Russia and Canada—all of them are going to be burning. We're in the midst of a great conflagration of forests, and that's unstoppable. The acidification of the oceans is also unstoppable. We'll lose all the coral, and all the fish. I actually think that we're probably going to lose ninety percent of the vertebrates and certainly most larger mammals. So, I don't know how to make sense of the term when you ask me what would be the most hopeful vision. Certainly, I guess, painlessly if we can somehow be taken out of our misery quickly so there's not a lot of suffering, so that mammals and humans die fairly rapidly, and we aren't evil to each other in the process. But as you said before, the powers that be—psychopathic and sociopathic heads of industry and corporations—are all about simple personal profit and corporate profit. They control the media waves. We're not going to get people out of denial because there's too much financial incentive to keep people there."

Jack: "So, what do you think is going to happen?"

Tom: "The kinds of breakthroughs that you, Jack, experienced in your community, real breakthroughs of human beings happen pretty regularly at 'the Dunbar number.' In communities under 150 and genuine tribes, there's a collective intelligence that emerges. Not just intelligent rationality, but heartful feelings. So, my hope is that there are pockets that survive. It's the fact that our species squandered our inheritance that we must wake up to. I would love it if there were seven thousand pockets of a 150 people, scattered in habitable places around the planet, that learn to live in relationship again to God, to life, to Reality, and enough mammals and vertebrates survive that we keep some biodiversity."

Jack: "Well, what would happen if there were another couple of pandemics?"

Tom: "That's a very real possibility. And if that happened, it could happen quickly—that'd be preferable to having billions of people starve to death over a period of some months."

Jack: "Oh my God. It's wild. The way you describe it, who do you think is going to survive?"

Tom: "I and most of my loved ones won't make it to the year 2030."

Jack: "Wow."

Tom: "Sometimes that breaks my heart, but mostly I just live with the sense that I've been given a terminal diagnosis. I'm committed to living fully loving my life and being a blessing to others and a contribution to my neighbors and my family—and trusting mortality. But yeah, I don't think my granddaughter will reach the age of twenty. I don't think she'll even reach the age of ten. But I'm committed that she has the best life possible for as long as possible."

Jack: "Well, what do you think of Elon Musk? Why aren't those guys waking up?"

Tom: "Because they're in techno-idolatry. They don't understand the nature of technology. When you actually step back and understand the history of technology, from spears and fire, any technology that benefits humans that doesn't benefit the living world, or that actively destroys the living world, always causes more problems for humans. It just does it over time. And religion has failed us because the definition of religion is to make sure that the present doesn't stop the future, and what existential means is that religion has failed. We have to completely leave religion behind."

Let's sit in Silence of Presence and fully embrace the tragic.

The speaker here, Tom—the name I gave him—was deeply influenced by another close colleague, a well-known evolutionary Buddhist ecologist, who was part of a larger circle of Doomers, many of whom were once at the center of the Human Potential movement but have now given up hope. There's an entire conversation going on in the world among people who have actually taken this very seriously. They basically say that those holding an optimistic viewpoint are totally naïve and are not looking at the facts.

So let's face the tragic full on. We're not going to avoid it.

1.7

THE FIRST AND THE SECOND SHOCKS OF EXISTENCE

Now we're going to go deeper. One of the ways you can experience this is to imagine *the first and second shocks of existence*. The first shock of existence is the experience of the death of the human being. Imagine we're in the hunter-gatherer era, before the dawn of human civilization. People are dying all the time, but we haven't yet experienced death *existentially*. Death is a biological fact, but it's not yet an existential fact.

At a certain moment we take death in existentially. When that happened is not clear. Some archaeologists suggest it happened at the beginning of the horticultural era, when elemental farming tools were first used, when we gained some stability by staving off the immediate threat of starvation— there was more time, and that deepened our realization of our mortality.

We realized we had more of a banquet—but "the skull still grins in at the banquet," in William James' evocative phrase. That's the existential realization of death. That first shock of existence essentially catapults the human being into their interiority, presses us inside, and also presses us outwards into the external world. It unleashes our best and worst, the greatest, most wondrous and most destructive forces of culture and Spirit.

All of civilization as we know it emerges from this realization. This was Ernest Becker's main point in *The Denial of Death*. **All of culture and civilization, the best of times and the worst of times, emerges as a response to this first shock of existence**. And then we go through all the stages of techno-economic human development: from horticultural to agrarian to early farming with plows drawn by oxen or horses, the different levels of agriculture through to the early industrial age, then the late industrial, and, relatively recently, to the information age.

Now we're moving into a hyper-informational period where the entire planet becomes one informational nervous system animated by biotech, nanotech, and infotech, in which we're all little cells in a larger technocracy. These levels of development of the human world have been unleashed as a response to the first shock of existence.

This brings us to the second shock of existence, which is the potential death of all of humanity. In the exchange between Tom and Jack, you can get a sense of this. They sent me this conversation to clue me into where their thinking was headed. The depth of this Doomer perspective has roots in William Catton's book *Overshoot*, and a whole host of other well-reasoned sources, which basically say that ecology is going to trump evolution.

If you aren't shocked, then you weren't reading carefully enough—with all due respect. If you *were* shocked then you just had a direct, non-conceptual experience of what we're calling the second shock of existence, *the potential death of the entire human species*.

The first shock of existence is the death of the individual human being.

The second shock of existence is the potential death of humanity.

1.8

SITTING IN THE TRAGIC—FACING APOCALYPSE: LOVE OR DEATH

Now, we're going deeper into the tragic. We simply must do this to eventually arrive at the post-tragic.

- We're going to get to unimaginable joy.
- We're going to get unimaginable pleasure.
- We're going to get to unimaginable love.
- We're going to get to the cherubs passionately embraced in the fullest Eros as we stand before potential destruction—the destruction of the temple of our planet, the temple of our earth—*we're going to see our way through.*

I deeply trust that Tom is incorrect for a lot of reasons. But we've got to take him seriously. We can't glibly dismiss him, because it's not just about Tom, but about an entire group of very serious people looking at very compelling information.

We're in this conversation in order to move through the grief because I think Stephen Jenkinson was incorrect when he said that grief and hope oppose each other. I think he has a deep understanding, but hope and grief are not oppositional. That's a false polarity. What does it mean to move beyond polarization? The question is: **How do I be skillfully hopeless, filled with hope, and beyond hope—all at the same time?**

There's a lot of wisdom in recent books like Benjamin Bratton's *The Stack* and Ramez Naam's *The Infinite Resource,* but they both get a lot of things wrong. Quite understandably, they partake in the huge mistakes being made in this current postmodern moment. There's a widespread sense in our culture that there can be no ground for value—and I think correcting that mistake can literally change everything. That's what the Great Library of CosmoErotic Humanism[1] is all about. It's what *Homo Amor,* the fulfilment of Homo sapiens, is about.

Stay with me in the tragic. Can you feel the desire to move beyond the tragic? We need to face apocalypse, the "unveiling"—there's something that needs to be revealed here. We can't genuinely disclose *Homo Amor* through a bypass road. There's no spiritual bypass here.

I was privileged to write a book called *Mystery of Love* back in 2001— an early version of a later book we called *A Return to Eros*—and the introduction is called *Love or Die.* What I tried to say there is very simple:

We have two choices: love or die.

I think that's still true, but we must understand what that means. We can't say it as a mere declaration. What does love mean? What does Eros mean? What does it mean to say that it's a structure of Reality? How do we establish and communicate that?

In *Mystery of Love,* I wrote about the term "avoidance," and I re-punctuated it, which is a practice in the interior sciences. So, instead of reading it as *avoidance* we read it as "a-void-dance." *We dance around the void.*

---

[1] CosmoErotic Humanism is a world philosophical movement aimed at reconstructing the collapse of value at the core of global culture. Read more at worldphilosophyandreligion. org.

We dance around the void by being workaholics, we dance around the void by meditating, we also dance around the void by paying attention only to our small world and even being in great integrity in it—which is beautiful. But to only be in integrity in my world, my creativity, and asking how this serves me—that's dancing around the void. We've got to come together in a real way. **We've got to love each other *Outrageously, like* we've never loved each other before.**

We've got to generate a Unique Self Symphony—a kind that Reality has never seen before. And this is not only possible—*it's the nature of Reality.*

But let's bracket all that for now. Do you notice how we already want to jump beyond the tragic? It's hard to do this work, this necessary move. *We can't move to the post-tragic unless we sit deeply in the tragic.*

1.9

STRANGE SNAPSHOTS OF REALITY: THE INTERCONNECTED PLANETARY STACK

I want to look at a couple of strange snapshots of the world before we go deeper into the tragic, as a bridge to the tragic.

Benjamin Bratton writes of what he calls the "planetary stack" as a way of viewing the actual structure of the planet. It's hard to see the total structure of the planet—it's one of the challenges with existential risk today. The second shock of existence is our word for catastrophic risk and existential risk, which is difficult to see. When we say that AI, artificial intelligence, is a threat, most people don't know what that really means. We understand what a war is, and we can understand an enemy in the traditional sense. But what is artificial intelligence, and why is it probably the single-most important threat to the future of the planet—even more so than the climate change risk Tom was talking about?

Part of Bratton's work is to understand the planetary stack, by exploring these questions:

1. What are the webs of algorithms that weave the planet together?
2. What is the computer web?
3. What is the cell phone web, and how is it monitored?

4. How do algorithms work?
5. What are the directions given to the system that will be self-fulfilling?

In 2015, Bratton gave a interesting talk called "Geobiopolitics and Planetary-Scale Computation."[2] I'm going to read and paraphrase some sections from it. "There's a planetary-scale computation," he says, meaning "the entire system of the planet is joined by a nervous system of Turing machines"— which is another way of saying computers. There are "networks of many billions of little Turing machines, including iPhones. **These Turing machines basically intake and absorb the earth's very chemistry in order to function.**"

He continues: "The stack is a hungry machine, and its curated population of algorithms, the algorithms that run the entire planetary stack, have no mass. Nonetheless, they are processing, they're eating, they're consuming the earth, and there's a mechanical appetite that's not mathematical. But it's real and it changes things on the ground, all the time, in all sorts of ways."

Then he gives an example: "This is made clear by unpacking and shifting through the hardware on which the stack depends. So, the computational stack, the planetary stack, depends on hardware, and one of the dimensions of hardware is silicon." Hence the name of California's tech center, Silicon Valley.

"But silicon is far from the only important substance required in manufacturing and maintaining the stack. The stack needs more exotic elements, and that need is intense. Even relatively simple consumer electronics and cloud tethers"—or what we call cell phones—"contain dozens of different minerals and metals that are sourced and extracted from every continent on earth, and some crucial metals are drawn largely from the rich and vulnerable mines in Central Africa, for example in the east of the Democratic Republic of Congo. Just as one example, there are big

---

[2] Benjamin Bratton, "Geobiopolitics and Planetary-Scale Computation: Sensors, Abstractors, Governors," talk given in Amsterdam at Sonic Arts Festival, February 28 2015, https://www.youtube.com/watch?v=8uVyvRdLn98.

chunks and little pebbles of tantalum or coltan, cassiterite, tin, wolframite, tungsten, and gold that are pulled by hand from cold, sludgy mountain rivers often by children living in what amounts to slavery, and eventually they make their way into the device component supply chain."

A number of years back, when they did some stats on this, "there were a few mines there in the East Congo that produced thirteen percent of the world's coltan, an inert metal used in tiny capacitors on our cell phones—from the same land from where the Belgians took the ivory and the Americans took the cobalt. Now, billions of human beings everywhere carry little bits of Africa around them in their pockets."

He continues: "The financial rewards of mining and trading in electronics has contributed to devastating effects in the region, including overlapping civil wars there and in Rwanda." In one study from 1998, upwards of five million people were brutally killed in the Congolese civil war, making it one of the deadliest conflicts since World War II. At the center of the conflict was the extraction and export of these minerals, both legal and illegal, which has been controlled and taxed by competing mafias and militias. These groups continue to terrorize local populations and use the proceeds of this export trade of coltan to finance their ongoing operations.

That's just a snapshot of Reality—we're carrying around a little piece of Africa in our cell phones right now, but we look away. I use my cell phone all the time, but I don't place my attention on where it came from. And indeed, **attention is hijacked in a thousand different ways**.

Society is structured as an attention economy to hijack your attention, which is the opposite of Eros, or love. Love is the placing of attention.

To be *Homo amor* is to be a unique incarnation of the Eros of Reality itself, to be an Outrageous Lover, an evolutionary lover, to have the love of evolution move through me. There's a full set of oral essays from 2018 and 2019, one on Outrageous Love and one on the Intimate Universe, that unpack the deep interior and exterior sciences behind these sentences.[3] To be a lover, to be *Homo amor*, to be a unique expression and incarnation of the LoveIntelligence of Cosmos, means "to place your attention." Love, or Eros, is the placing of attention. Sex is love in the body, so sex is the placing of radical attention on other.

We have a legitimate and sacred need for attention. We're healed by attention. Reality needs our attention. **That which blooms Reality, at every level from matter to life to mind, is attention.** *Attention blooms Reality.*

But we've displaced our attention. We have no idea that the cell phone in my pocket comes from African coltan, which has directly and indirectly caused millions and millions of deaths—unpoliced, unregulated, unseen. *No, that's not worth placing our attention on…*

REALITY IS EROS, REALITY IS INTIMACY

Let's think about cars for a second. One of the challenges today is that every advance, each solution to a problem creates a *new* set of problems. For example, at one point we had massive problems with the widespread use of horses in society: too much horse manure lying around, causing every manner of disease and a host of other problems. We "solved" that problem with the internal combustion engine, with automobiles that gradually evolved.

But, of course, we know all about the wars of the twentieth century and the horrors they inflicted, mangling hundreds of millions of human bodies. They were all dependent on the internal combustion engine, which, within a couple of short decades, became the carriage of war, unleashing unimaginable levels of destruction. Solving one problem, in this case horse husbandry, created another problem. Not to mention what the burning of

---

[3] See: *Our First Steps as Homo Amor: Becoming the New Human and the New Humanity* (Integral Publishers, 2023), and *Mythologize, Don't Pathologize: Living Your Sacred Autobiography* (Integral Publishers, 2023).

fossil fuels does to our planet. **That's the nature of the planetary stack. Everything is interconnected with everything else, and to see the interconnections requires a great placing of attention.**

When we don't see the interconnections, then we're utterly confused about what to do and how to act. That's part of one of the generator functions for the second shock of existence, what we might call "the hyperobject of Reality." *Hyperobject*, a term coined by Timothy Morton, points to the incomprehensible complexity of certain aspects of Reality, like capitalism and climate change, large systems connected to all other systems. Indeed, we can rephrase this to point to **the Eros of Intimacy that defines Reality, the Eros of the Intimate Universe that connects everything at the human level.**

Each of the thirty-seven trillion cells in the human body are connected to all the others. There's a complete awareness of the radical intimacy of the human body, and there's a non-local, intimate relationship between all the cells of the body. It's shocking. And that's just one example of the Intimate Universe in the human body. Every part knows its impact on all the others, and when they don't, we call that cancer. **Cancer is when one part moves and grows but is unaware of their impact on the planetary stack.** For the organism to be healthy, we need every cell to be healthy. But in the self-reflective human world we've generated through technology—because technology is the explosion of *exterior* interconnectivity—we've generated interconnected systems that are unaware of each other, so that everything is affecting everything else with devastating consequences, generating both catastrophic and existential risk. What does this mean?

There's a virus going around—whether it was intentionally manufactured as a bioweapon that escaped, or was a result of gain-of-function research organized between the United States and China that was intentionally deployed, or whether it was a result of open wet markets where brutalized animals are served up as meat. However it happened, because of the interconnected world system and the planetary stack, a problem in Wuhan has now killed millions of people.

It's all interconnected.

I'll give you one last snapshot just to feel the strangeness of our world. What does it mean that more people are killed by car accidents than all the terrorist actions in the world put together? What is the calculation we make, in the State of Israel, for example, where car accidents have killed twice as many people as all the wars. If we would just, for example, lower the speed limit by x amount, we would reduce those deaths dramatically. But we don't. Why? What's the calculation of modernity? Why is it okay to have mangled bodies, widows, orphans, funerals, in order to drive ten miles faster? Why is no one objecting to it? That was just an interlude—a snapshot of the strangeness of our world.

CONTEMPLATIVE EXERCISE: INTEGRATING THE TRAGIC AND THE SECOND SHOCK OF EXISTENCE

Take a few minutes to reflect about coltan or the Congo or car accidents and the interconnected world—or any topics related to the second shock.

How is the tragic hitting you in this moment?

How are you updating your model of the world?

How are you experiencing and feeling it in your body?

How are you understanding the second shock of existence?

How hard is it to stay engaged with this? Do you notice any defenses, distractions, avoidant tendencies?

How are you internalizing and integrating this sensibility?

Write down any insights you might have. Or perhaps consider calling a friend to discuss with them.

1.10

DEEP DIVE INTO THE TRAGIC, PART 1: THE 2020s, THE CURRENT TRAGIC STATE OF AFFAIRS

Let's go all the way now, deeper into the tragic—we're not turning away—in order that we get to the other side, to the post-tragic. The only way out is through. Let us hold this together for the sake of evolving the source code:

- The evolution of culture and consciousness.
- The genuine evolution of love.
- The emergence of *Homo amor*.
- The fulfillment of *Homo sapiens*.
- The only way to move from the tragic to the post-tragic.

Let's move from the necessary but insufficient meta-theoretical discussions of the tragic, the interconnected planetary stack and the Doomer conversation between Jack and Tom, to a more direct sense of what the second shock is. It's critical to understand that the second shock of existence won't happen all at once. It's more likely a slowly building series of shocks you barely know are happening. Covid is the first of a series of such shocks.

A shock, as the dictionary defines it, is "a seemingly sudden, utterly surprising blow to the mind, body, and heart which creates disorientation and confusion." But then you go on, you forget it happened. We adjust and get back to *business as usual*. It's precisely in that sense that Covid is a shock—it invokes the spectrum of sudden rupture, which creates apparently catastrophic change, which we then get used to very rapidly.

Shocks also occur in economies, such as an oil price shock, a rupture in the stable structure of supply and demand structures, prices, or resource availability. **The particular nature of a societal shock, of apocalypse, reveals to the naked eye what was once under the carpet before the shock.** The fault lines that could be ignored before, now come to the surface with clarity, and they cause great suffering. For example, in the early days of Covid in Italy and the United States, many doctors and nurses died because there weren't masks available. How could it be that Italy, a developed country in the European Union surrounded by other developed countries, and the United States, the preeminent industrial giant in the world, didn't have enough masks, such that doctors and nurses were dying in pain on ventilators?

The world has been built to optimize win-lose metrics based on particular kinds of supply chains that maximize profit in the short term, in which contracts are structured in a way that only certain people are allowed to sell to other people based on certain incentives and exchanges. The masks being made in the global industrial economy weren't being made locally in the United States or in Italy, so the supply chains broke. Paradoxically, most of the supply chains were in China, where Covid originated.

You've got this strange situation in which the post-World War II world—reorganized during the great gathering at Bretton Woods in 1944—is structured upon interconnected supply chains. **We reorganized the world to ensure that nation-states should never fight with each other again because we had developed our first existential weapon: the nuclear bomb, which had the capacity to destroy the whole world.** We intertwined the whole world through supply chains enabling global economic exchange, so that to bomb another country would be to bomb your own supply chain. That was part of the resetting of the world order, which was meant to create world peace. And partly it has worked—there hasn't been another world war, though there have been proxy wars (where a country fights through other countries).

Seventy-five years after Bretton Woods, the level of existential risk in the world has grown exponentially, based on multiple factors. As an example: Superpowers with nuclear weapons can be monitored, and the uranium needed to enrich a bomb virtually requires an entire nation-state to generate it. It's available only in particular places, and it can be easily monitored. However, we increasingly have multiple platforms capable of delivering nuclear payloads, owned and directed by a plethora of countries, as well as non-state actors.

This means that the mutually assured destruction which formed the basis of deterrence between the United States and Russia doesn't work anymore, and all the nuclear stockpiles still exist. What happens when the world moves towards greater and greater instability based on many other existential risks, while all of that payload material is fully available and deliverable?

That's just one of ten or so current existential risks, to get a sense of the potential proximity of the second shock of existence.

· · ·

Covid is an example where we see the fragility of a world that has been optimized for efficiency, but not for safety. The supply chains didn't break down, but they almost did. Maybe more accurately: they didn't break down in the developed world, though they did break down in major parts of Africa.

The direct cascading effects of Covid, even just in terms of economic devastation, are unimaginable. But the virus is a first shock, likely one of many, and its impacts will be with us throughout the 2020s. It will take even the most resilient economies much of the decade to return to normal. **When we look back at the early 2020s, we're going to remember that the impulse to return to normal was intense.** There's an overwhelming desire to cover up the yawning void that's been disclosed by the realization that it's not all *too big to fail*—glimpses of what we just called the second shock.

Even when these effects aren't directly seen, they're felt like the tremors of an earthquake all over the world. People are desperate to calm the tremors and to turn away from what they glimpsed for a moment. Many people around the world have been financially, emotionally, and physically devastated. In the early 2020s, people did what they could to pick up the pieces of their lives and the lives of those near and dear to them. The pressure of present survival, of grief and despair, often blocked people's ability to even see the future. Many broke down, many collapsed, many who were barely holding it together simply couldn't anymore.

But for those who were relatively untouched by the pandemic, the lockdowns became a distant memory. You dusted it off and talked about it at a party or in comic routines in a movie. The fortunate felt themselves safe *because they were split off from their shared identity.* **They were cut off from intimacy, which we define in our intimacy equation as:** *shared identity in the context of relative otherness, times mutuality of recognition, mutuality of pathos, mutuality of value, and mutuality of purpose.* The very fortunate, those who somehow got through Covid untouched, said, "Wow, this is the best time I've ever had"—they were split off from their shared identity, and from their shared pathos with those who suffered. In some corners of the financial world, many predatory opportunists had a field day. That's what it looks like in the 2020s.

• • •

Looking ahead, throughout the 2020s, the United States, Europe, and much of Asia will try to reassert their normalcy. But underneath, all sorts of structural changes are taking place—with devastating effect. This return to "normal" is expressed in increases in consumption. Win-lose metrics continue to govern the world narrative. It's the Success Story 2.0: *I achieve, I consume, I have status, I'm recognized for my status.* Contrast this with the premodern Success Story 1.0: *I'm successful if I'm obedient to God.*

So modernity's win-lose metrics state: "I've achieved, I've stood out, I've won in the competition, I've generated something that gets me paid and brings me status." This goes wild in the world during the 2020s. The leaders of India, China, and Russia, as well as those in Western democracies see the **consumption of more and more goods by their citizens to be the essential measure of personal and collective success**, as well as essential for the consolidation of political power. As such, in the 2020s the consumption of more and more goods becomes virtually synonymous with the return to normalcy.

But this excessive consumption across the globe is now driven by a new market force unlike anything that's ever been imagined in the history of the world, what Benjamin Bratton calls a "new epidermis," a new skin that extends around the globe: a worldwide nervous system of ubiquitous computing, based on the Internet of Things, in which everyone is implicated. This largely invisible web is driven by the leading edge of sophisticated artificial intelligence, animated by new forms of machine learning—and leading us towards constant, massive consumption. It was initially developed by Google, and a little bit later by Facebook, later followed by Microsoft, Verizon, and Amazon—and all the other tech giants are scrambling for a piece of the action.

For example, the public mission of Facebook and Google is connecting the world and organizing the world's information. But that's a utopian smokescreen for a far more insidious business model based on data mining. As Eric Schmidt, the former CEO of Google, said: *data is the new oil.* **The real business model of Facebook, Google and this entire system is not to sell your data.** Mark Zuckerberg in an interview a few months ago said, "We don't sell data." Of course, this is the best way to lie—by sort of telling the truth. **Their business model is to collect as much data**

on you as possible, based on every single thing you do on the web. For example, let's say that you see an ad that has a brown cat, and then there's an ad that comes up ninety seconds later, and the ad has a certain kind of font and then it's followed by two seconds of music, and then there's another message with a different font, a different cat, and slightly different music, and then you're asked to buy something. All your responses are being tracked—how long you linger with each sequence, for example—to know what most effectively captures your attention. That's just a random example.

Each particular sequence helps both create and identify you as part of a what's called a "peer group," which is not a group of lawyers, or musicians, or dentists you're a part of. Rather, it's a euphemism for categorizing people so they can be more effectively manipulated through a particular sequence. Facebook and Google do it every day through algorithms that are self-generating and exponential.

This means that algorithms are able to train themselves to get better and better at what they do: trying to keep you on the site for as long as possible, either to get you to make a decision or to gather data about you. If it gets you to make a decision based on a particular sequence, then it notes that in order to optimize for how others in your peer group will make that decision, making subtle changes to increase effectiveness: change the font, replace the brown cat with a white one, change the music, etc. The algorithm is constantly split-testing in this way, creating and cataloging peer groups, subconsciously appealing to them, encouraging them to do particular things. So, strictly speaking, the data is not sold—*instead, the predictive analysis about what peer groups will do is sold to third-parties.* That's a lucrative business model.

They want to keep you on the web for as long as possible, and they do that by hijacking your attention. This is best achieved through negativity, clickbait, and other subtle, sophisticated strategies deployed by algorithms designed to capture your attention. No one intentionally decides to go on Facebook and stay there for six hours, but there's a bottomless well of attention hijacking designed to garner as much data about you—and not just by what you do. How long your mouse hovers before you click is a piece of data in your peer group. Everything—visible and invisible—how you type, the order of your typing, the spacing of your typing, is fed into machine intelligence which **creates data about how to get you to act not according to your highest Self,** *Homo amor,* **but according to the** *lowest common denominator* **of your peer group.**

That's the core business model of Google and Facebook: the product is predictive analysis that reaches virtual certainty.

This is not advertising as usual. It's about how to prompt you to make decisions in the real world that you wouldn't otherwise make, including prompting you how to vote. Eric Schmidt, the head of Google in 2008 and 2012, ran Barack Obama's Facebook campaign, which targeted undecided voters based on—apparently—a knowledge of precisely what prompts they were vulnerable to. In 2016, one of Schmidt's lieutenants worked for a company in London called Cambridge Analytica that was hired by the Trump campaign to do some version of the same thing.

While there's a lot of uncertainty about exactly what Cambridge Analytica did, what's clear is that it wasn't exceptional. It was *business as usual,* unseen by the public, that was briefly exposed—and this kind of manipulation is used by legacy structures, which pretend to tell us everything that is going on.

Are we really deciding, are we really choosing, are we really even voting? What's actually driving our democracies?

All those things are happening in the backdrop of the 2020s, as we create a world wide web whose core motive and pattern is not to connect people or make the world's information available, but to attract data, which is then translated and sold to third-parties in order to generate excessive, superficial consumption and windfall wealth for tech elites that somehow don't pay taxes. **The world wide web becomes not a story of Eros, the actual Intimate Universe, but a tale of pseudo-eros, *full of sound and fury,* generating no Value.**

It creates a downward spiral as negativity generates further "engagement," a euphemism for the hijacking of your attention on the web. This means you lack the attention to place in your inward space to generate true love, to generate the emergence of who you actually are, to generate the construction of Self.

Emptiness, depression, and anxiety become part of a worldwide mental disorder rooted in a usurping of Eros by pseudo-eros. That pseudo-eros, that emptiness, those levels of artificially motivated obsessive consumption drive the world's exponential growth curve, and that growth curve itself drives the global extraction model.

Like all destructive exponential growth curves, you eventually hit planetary boundaries, and you can no longer run a linear materials economy.

1.11

DEEP DIVE INTO THE TRAGIC, PART 2: THE 2030s, THE CLIMATE SHOCK

The shock of Covid in the 2020s is followed by desperate but seemingly futile attempts to return to normal. That's the first level of collapse. The ongoing coronavirus pandemic throws hundreds of millions of people into functional poverty. People struggle to rebuild. *Homo amor* and **First Values and First Principles are not resourced. They don't enter the world, and a new worldview fails to take hold.**

In this time between worlds and time between stories, no New Story of Value was developed and delivered into Reality.

Then everyone's hit by the next level of shock: climate shock. It's not a one-time shock, but like everything we're describing here, is an incremental process. We gradually get used to it day by day until one day it all comes together, it all collapses, and we wake up to the full impact of all these discrete events. We're devastated by the full extent of the shock. **Just like the pandemic shock, the awareness of climate disaster moves in waves: it appears, it recedes, it thunders, it whispers, then it crashes our lives**

as we know them on the shores of devastating but fully predictable destruction.

This is but one scenario where the climate collapse predicted by science explodes into our daily lives. What might it actually look like in the 2030s? Let's take the United States as an example, but realize it plays out in different ways around the world. Remember that in the United States most people are already living paycheck to paycheck. Most people die in debt with no tangible assets to leave to the next generation. Take a look at the economic impact of the average family's ability to quite literally put food on the table and a roof over their heads. An average family currently pays something like a quarter of their income for utilities: water, electricity, insurance, and so forth. And another half of their income goes to rent or mortgage payments.

What will happen when the costs of climate crisis land directly on your shoulders? Fast forward a decade, when the world's running out of water, clean air, livable temperatures. Guess which bills suddenly spike? Your water bill is now 25 percent of your income, and your electricity bill—because you have to run air conditioning day and night—comes to another 20 percent. **Now you're in total, perpetual, unpayable debt.**

One day you get a letter from your insurance company. Your home insurance premium is going up by fifty percent a year because of the increasing risk of fire, flood, and earthquakes. You feel a sudden surge of panic. Your income has been stuck for most of your life—all your credit cards are maxed out. How can you afford this, what can you do? In the 2020s, mega-fires and mega-floods raged out of control, sea levels rise, land burns. The burning and flooding of houses and neighborhoods, residential and industrial, are already regular events on the news.

In the 2020s, people are on lockdown—they can't leave their homes.

In the 2030s, huge swaths of people actually *lose* their homes to fires and floods.

In the 2020s, Covid and its direct and indirect impacts cause people to lose their jobs. Lots of people give up working, but for the many who don't, all of their energy is poured into the desperate struggle to retrain themselves and find new jobs.

In the 2030s, there are simply no jobs to be had. Entire geographic areas—from neighborhoods to cities, even whole regions—are forced to close down due to extreme weather patterns, flooding from rising tides and fires.

In the 2020s, societies grind to a complete halt on and off, through a series of pandemic shocks. Governments step in and artificially keep broken economies barely afloat.

In the 2030s, governments no longer have the capacity to bail out economies. Indeed, economies as we know them effectively cease to exist. Banks, insurance companies, and mutual funds see their holdings plunge in value. Many, if not most, go bankrupt. The savings of the larger sectors of society, including the whole middle class, are burned and washed away. What happens then? This in turn of course causes waves of small businesses to shut down, and this in turn generates a massive new wave of unemployment.

The dry cleaner is closed—sorry, those chemicals are now unaffordable. Breweries and butchers shut their doors—who could afford beer or meat anymore anyways? Water cannot be used for pleasure when we need it to quell the raging fires. Who's going to insure shops? Rents are out of control. No business is left unaffected. Productivity falls, incomes collapse. Who knows how to make ends meet? Industrial civilization can no longer employ people in a world now increasingly unable to support basic life.

In the 2020s, people survived the coronavirus depression by taking on debt and selling their assets, homes, saving bonds, retirement funds.

In the 2030s, they don't have any of those left. Anyways, there are no real buyers. Who wants to buy your home? Who wants to give you credit now? The financial system can't cope with the risks of climate change to begin with. As insurance companies go bankrupt, taking banks and funds with

46

them, what savings and investments people once had, have imploded. Worse, there is nobody to turn to for credit or debt or insurance—or much employment at all.

In the 2020s, cash and gold coins ruled. It was the only thing left worth having, if you could get any. When the financial infrastructure of a society collapsed in on itself, the core of the middle class—small- and medium-sized businesses—collapsed with it.

In the 2030s, there's no one to guarantee the credit and debt that has become a survival need, particularly as prices spiral out of control because of the scarcity of supply. The average person has no access to any sort of working capital. The chasm between the elites, the haves, and the have-nots widens to a breaking point, and the world is literally in a new caste system. The ultra-rich can afford augmentation, they can afford CRISPR genetic surgeries and neural implants.

For centuries the rich thought they were smarter and more beautiful than everyone else, but it was nonsense. Now it begins to be true. Cosmetic surgeries and enhanced cognitive augmentations are available to the elite. The rest of society is at a breaking point, making the Indian caste system look like a joke. All the remaining energy of society is poured into trying to rebuild what's been destroyed. That's what happened in the 2020s—homes, medical centers, schools, and universities. But now there's no energy for any new building. People's lives have collapsed.

We can't get to the post-tragic, we can't re-formulate Reality, we can't evolve the source code, we can't move the next step from *Homo sapiens* to *Homo amor*, unless we can walk through the tragic—and yes, it's brutal.

***The tragic is brutal*. That's the nature of the tragic.**

People's lives collapse in this version of the 2030s—basic human needs like education, housing, and healthcare—a titanic struggle in the 2020s for so many—now become impossible to afford for most. The old notion of a workplace has all but disappeared. Human identity is more confused than it's ever been. **Unique Self never made it into the world. The Center for World Philosophy and Religion, the Office for the Future, and the Unique Self Institute were never properly resourced.**

Human identity is more confusing than it's ever been. There are no deeper First Values and First Principles, no shared Universal Grammar of Value. Extreme depression sets in across society. The core structure of depression, is a sense of futility—meaning, "I can't change anything." A radical sense of powerlessness. **Powerlessness is a poison that permeates human hearts.**

The only job is to find some desperate way to put food on the table tomorrow. As climate shock tears entire economies apart, people will become something much more like nomadic traders.

The middle class has disappeared, the stable lives of jobs fixed in time and space, with fixed salaries—it's all gone. Today you might be able to get this gig in this city, and tomorrow you might be able to sell a pallet of that on Amazon, and another day you might get some work someplace else. Life becomes a game of survival. Many resort to scavenging for dwindling resources atop the landfill of industrial society, selling to those who need them even more desperately.

The core stability of life that allows not only for human dignity, but for sanity, goes up in smoke. Of course, without First Values and First Principles, the stability of life disappears, as do the institutions of society. The imperatives of family are not considered to be rooted in intrinsic value. They're called by Yuval Harari "social constructions."

Family, education, the transfer of culture from generation to generation—all that has melted away, swept aside by the immediate imperative of survival. Sex between two live persons comes to be seen as a foolhardy risk. The black market for extreme pornography proliferates, being the only thing that could—for a desperate, fleeting, pathetic, desperate moment—shock people out of their trance. As more degraded forms of pornography run rampant, so too do social forms of pornography on social media explode, ever more cruelly and virulently. Twitter mobs spout mindless chatter online all the time, without anyone realizing that their inner experience is being hacked to construct data personality profiles being sold to the highest bidder.

All of it is encouraged, commodified, and monetized by the smiling leaders of the tech plex,[4] who are themselves hidden away, living in guarded and gated communities. **Trust rooted in intimacy has all but disappeared** and yet, in the masses of population, people are forced together in sloppy, slovenly, painful, often violent, unbearable pseudo-intimacies. Sloppy, degraded forms of communal living become the norm, animated not by the social visions or ideals of the *kibbutz*, but out of dire necessity. The global intimacy disorder shifts into overdrive, while core human experiences of meaning, purpose, pathos, nobility, honor, loyalty, and joy seem sadly unavailable—or unimaginable—to most people.

All these fault lines, already beginning to show up in the 2020s, are now cracking wide open. Certainly, First Values and First Principles—ideas in which every generation participates in the evolution of consciousness which is the evolution of love—no longer have any soil in which to root. **Experiences of radical aliveness and Eros become ever more rare pockets of isolated peak experience.** They're never the fabric of the average person's daily life, as a surplus of powerlessness gradually de-eroticizes most lives. The handmaidens of Eros—creativity, innovation, transformation—are words well on the way to becoming obsolete in the 2020s, and are largely unutterable by the 2030s.

---

[4] By tech plex we mean the technological infrastructure of society, which includes the entire "planetary stack" (Benjamin Bratton's term), as well as the daily immersive environment constituted by social media and the internet of things. The tech plex is unique in that it has facilitated a new world in which technology is no longer a tool, but an immersive environment. We live inside of that plex. That plex moves all the way up and all the way down the planetary stack. The tech plex is constituted by infrastructure, social structure, and superstructure, as we have previously defined these terms. Clearly, there's infrastructure, in terms of the actual physical structures of the tech plex. There's social structure, in relationship to the laws that govern and the absence of laws in relationship to the tech plex. And third, there's superstructure. That is to say, the technology actually codifies particular values and ignores or bypasses or rejects other values. The tech plex is not value-neutral; the tech plex implies a set of worldviews or superstructures.

Those who could have contributed to the articulation of First Values and First Principles looked away—everybody got caught up in their lives. **The privileged failed to turn privilege into responsibility, to take a seat at the table of history.**

The result: we entered the 2030s without a coherent vision of the New Human and the New Humanity. It's only such a vision that has the capacity to fuel genuine transformation and evolution in times of crisis. But this energy is absent in the 2030s. It's just not available.

Instead of going global, politics re-tribalize, descending into the depths of polarization that makes the 2020s look like a lovefest. **Authoritarian regimes take root all over the world, as the demonization of the other becomes standard.** Racism, which we thought we'd moved beyond, moves directly back to center stage. So do cancel-culture mobs which seem to espouse Eros on the surface, but are almost always manipulated by power-players behind the scenes.

- Governments lack any real power, and no institutions are trusted.
- Voting is seen as helpless, and vigorous democracy is a relic of the past.
- Words seem to lose their meaning.
- Love and liberty, the vows we thought were worth dying for, are no longer self-evidently understood.
- Everything is experienced as levels of simulation and artifice.
- No institutions are trusted.
- There seems to be no direct access to the real.
- Only rage seems real—and even that is hijacked and commodified by the tech plex.
- Core values like loyalty disappear, as win-lose metrics hyper-intensify.
- Core human experiences like joy, care, compassion, wonder, humor, and love fade from memory.

1.12

DEEP DIVE INTO THE TRAGIC, PART 3: THE 2040s, THE SIXTH MASS EXTINCTION SHOCK

As we move into the 2040s, even local governmental power disappears. Instead, all power is relocated upwards to a handful of mega-corporations who've captured the platforms to market whatever scarce goods are available. By now, *all* sales of goods, information, and communication take place within the tech plex, subject to the tech plex. It's the triumph of digital dictatorship, where there's **virtually no genuine personal interaction**—and therefore no recourse—no channel of appeal in cases of injustice. Digital mobs have some new economic power, which they begin to realize, and they only buy products that support their extreme views—any voices deemed "politically incorrect" are silenced by that economic power.

Again, it's critical to understand that **none of this happens in an instant.** Rather, it occurs as a daily onslaught of barely noticeable assaults on human dignity and value, that gradually—sometimes imperceptibly but unceasingly—creep in and expand. One day we wake up and then all of a sudden it's different than it ever was, often in terrifying ways.

Let's step deeper into this vision of the 2040s.

The second shock of existence is a series of cascading shocks.

- The 2020s saw the initial shock of the pandemic, with its direct and indirect ravages, and the shocking realizations that our systems *aren't* too big to fail.
- The 2030s saw the shock of climate change with its savage impact on jobs and the core structures of society.
- The 2040s brings the shock of the sixth mass extinction.

Like the pandemic shock and the climate shock, the extinction shock is gradual. It unfolds over months and years, maybe even decades—but is experienced as a shock unlike any other.

It simply becomes undeniable that nothing exists independently of everything else. We always knew this was somewhat true, but the interconnectivity of Reality is now clearly demonstrated in its exterior form by systems theory. Of course, what's happening now is that the core knowledge of interconnectivity exists only in exterior systems. What we experienced intensifying over the last decades is the demonstrable disclosure that we're fully interconnected in every way. Therefore, **when we fail to interconnect our interior systems—because our interior technologies, our social technologies, have stalled—we have no real collective intelligence.** We have no emergent order. So there are only two choices remaining: oppression or chaos: the former through the rise of autocratic societies like Russia and China, and the latter through the breakdown of prevailing systems.

The only alternative to oppression and chaos is a new emergent order, a new collective intelligence, *a new cultural enlightenment* that yields an emergent order based on a new story. For a decade, I've been calling it *the democratization of enlightenment*. Only this emergent order, based in this new story, can creates *an ethos for a global civilization*—based on a recognition that there *are* intrinsic values that we share, according to a universal grammar of value. When none of that's in place, all we have is the unbearable intimacy of a planet that's fully interconnected, and subject to the ultimately deadly nature *of our denial, our ignorance*, of that interconnectivity.

In other words, because of zero-sum rivalrous dynamics, we lose any sense of shared identity and intimacy in our interiors, and we're left only with the planetary stack of exponentially multiplying technological layers in which we're all—everything and everyone, every dimension of the physical world, every dimension of the lifeworld, and every dimension of the human world—fully and inextricably linked. Nothing is separate. But the widespread denial of this interconnectivity continues into the 2030s and the 2040s because there is no alternative vision, no new interior technology adequate to this time between worlds and time between stories.

The Renaissance generated universal human rights, and the seeds of feminism. It generated the scientific method, and other great *wonders and dignities*. However, while exterior technologies advanced exponentially, interior technologies stalled. **We're left with the interior technologies of the seventeenth and eighteenth century in a world that's unrecognizable on the exterior, and none of them are sufficient to address our world situation.**

The old *Homo sapiens*, based on win-lose metrics in a post-Bretton Woods world—in which exponential technology dominates Reality, in which we're part of a nervous system run by TechnoFeudalism[5], in which we've actually gone through pandemic shock and then climate shock—all of that denial and ignorance explodes in the 2040s.

In the sixth mass extinction, in the 2040s, we completely exterminate the very life upon which our own lives depend.

The most vulnerable, those with no voice to speak for themselves, are the first victims: insects, coral reefs, butterflies, bees—all these sentient, magical living beings upon whom we ecologically depend for life go ex-

---

[5] See forthcoming book, David J. Temple, *TechnoFeudalism: How Humanity Escapes the Global Skinner Box: Artificial Intelligence, TechnoFeudalism, & the Collapse of Value in the Digital Age.*

tinct first. They're followed by entire species of fish, birds, mammals, reptiles, and trees—those sentient beings that have been the base of the great ecological chains, go extinct. *Ecology trumps evolution.*

In the 2030s, the stability of the seasons as we know them finally disappears for good. In the 2040s, extinction shock builds on climate shock and pandemic shock. The foundation of the earth system is ripped away, and the great ecological edifices upon which they're built all collapse. It's fish that clean our rivers, and insects that turn the soil which grow our crops. **What happens when we have no river water that we can drink, and no crop that takes root because there's no healthy soil?** Deeply feel the tragedy of this version of the 2040s. As the temperature keeps rising, water and food are more scarce, and there's less oxygen as the trees die out. Whole ecosystems begin to collapse and tip over:

- Vast forests die and become deserts.
- Rivers turn dank and muddy.
- Lakes suddenly turn poisonous.
- Oceans gradually empty out and fill up with strange invaders.
- Topsoil itself turns to poison…

Nature itself seems to have gone topsy-turvy. Every month brings a fresh nightmare, a new surprise. What ecologists had worried about all along is happening, though by now no one really struggles to understand because it takes too much precious energy. The bottom has been ripped out of the ecosystems in a series of cascading collapses.

Food chains, water tables, raw materials, the very structure of life itself is now ripped away in the 2030s and 2040s. For all of the devastation of the 2020s, the basic structures of Reality—food chains, water tables, raw materials—all remained in place. In the 2030s, in the midst of climate shock, they begin to teeter and crumble. And in the 2040s, during an extinction shock, they completely implode, making the pandemic-shocked world of the 2020s look like the Garden of Eden.

In the 2040s, one harvest fails after another. The price of the few remaining foodstuffs, mostly rice and bread, shoots up even higher. The fish no longer cleanse the rivers and entire cities are left without water. Oceans that had once provided abundant nourishment are now full of inedible, parasitic biomass, or are simply vast dead zones. The raw materials which made the silicon and the steel that powered the screens humanity looked at are now inaccessible. **All of the great ecosystems begin to die off**, irreversibly: the Amazon and other rainforests, the oceans, the glaciers, and ice at the poles—all the great, interconnected systems that keep life on planet earth as we know it, breathing and thriving—including, of course, us.

- What happens when a harvest suddenly fails, a harvest upon which a whole continent depends?
- What happens when a river runs dry, one that whole countries depend on?
- What happens when the topsoil goes barren and there's no way to replenish it?
- What happens when the shore of an entire continent is suddenly invaded by a new species because the fish have all gone?

The climate shock of the 2030s disabled the effective operations of the financial and economic systems of society, but the extinction shock of the 2040s shatters even more fundamental systems. Medicine, water, and food systems are rendered unreliable or entirely dysfunctional. Extreme poverty sweeps planet earth, now completely divided into two fundamentally different castes. But even the rich are beginning to scramble for unadulterated food, clean air, and clean water. **Profound and terrible widespread suffering becomes the new normal.**

The extraction model that drove the exponential growth curves of the twentieth and early twenty-first centuries is finally falling off the cliff. That which is most elemental to life—oxygen, water, energy, medicine, and food—are no longer givens of Reality. All of the systems once dedicated to pricing, allocating, marketing, and managing them make little sense now.

Reality as we know it collapses all around us.

The word "unemployment" is a word that doesn't make sense any longer because it operates only in the context of employment. AI and advanced machine learning have greatly accelerated. Together with the cumulative effects of pandemic shock, climate shock, and extinction shock is the shock of no jobs for most of humanity. Most jobs are done by AI and machine intelligence. The overwhelming majority of human beings who don't have a job will probably never have a job again.

Put that together with the collapse of sexing, the collapse of reproduction from the previous decade, and you begin to get a very grim picture. What's even more ominous is that new versions of artificial intelligence have begun to trade with each other. The human being as consumer is now close to entirely unnecessary. In the nineteenth century and into the twentieth century, masses of humans, the new industrial workers, protested against exploitation. **In the 2030s and 2040s, exploitation is not the issue for the mass of humanity—it's complete *irrelevance*.**

Without First Values and First Principles, without Unique Self, without irreducible value—for most people the experience of not having a conventional job or family is virtually equivalent to death.

There is no other narrative of identity. In the 2040s, the negligence and arrogant postmodern dismissals of all grammars of value which took place in the late twentieth and early twenty-first centuries come home to roost with a vengeance to strike at the heart of the systems of life itself. Traditional relational structures have all broken down, and classical structures of work and reward are completely undermined. People are thrown into an **abyss of confusion and depression** unlike anything the world has ever known.

• • •

Ecology trumps evolution. There's a total sense of alienation from the one true sense of identity: "I am evolution in person." The word *Homo amor* never makes it into the vocabulary.

Without intimacy comes new pathology. The intimacy of exterior technology generates the new pathologies of modernity, which collapse us into the sixth mass extinction—and this collapse of identity gives rise to a dark tide of rage. The realization finally dawns that there is no shared value, and there can be no shared intimacy. There's rage at the failed systems. **But even worse than rage, there's a more horrific quality that poisons Reality—the sense of dead end, no exit, the stupor of extinction shock in which huge masses of the world's population realize there's no way to get our bearings, there's no orienting North Star of value to follow.** There seems to be no road home.

The tech elites, ostensibly for the sake of the masses they've exploited for decades, now cynically pretend to serve those masses. But even from their heavily guarded enclaves, they manipulate all of this to their own ends. Sectors of the population—whole towns, cities, and regions—begin to go hungry and thirsty. They become beggars, pleading for food from their neighbors, who themselves have little to give. The depth of discontent shatters whatever trust still lingers in the body politic. Finally, the veneer of civilization begins to entirely break down by the end of the 2040s, exploding into a wave of *Mad Max*-like violence that spreads across the globe, as everyone competes for resources now suddenly in desperately short supply.

Poverty leads to violence, just like it always does. **Work, jobs, employment, family, stability, security, truth, meaning, value—*they're all gone.*** Economic society, culture, politics, the bulwarks and pillars of civilization, have by now utterly collapsed, and we move closer towards digital dictatorship. The promise of health and security is used to induce people to wear biometric sensors, which allow for even more data collection and even more control. Lockdowns strip away what's left of civil liberties. Public gatherings are outlawed, and the human creative ferment is removed from society, with obvious insidious results.

Let's take the very last step—under-the-skin surveillance. We move from *holdables* to *wearables*. Everything you feel is able to be tracked. Feelings are hacked through biometric sensors, and algorithms are used to predict who will and who won't commit a crime. In many former democracies, authoritarianism takes over, overtly replacing the charade of democracy. The tech plex reigns supreme, regional wars over scarce survival resources break out around the world. Resources wars govern our everyday lives.

I know this is painful to listen to... *Why won't he just shut the fuck up? Shut up, Gafni. I don't want to hear this anymore.* But we need to stay with it just a bit more...

Labor in the traditional forms we know of is a distant memory, like democracy itself. Now work is seen as reporting for service, going to war, strategizing a way to gain this basic resource from a society that once used to be an ally. For the lucky few, employment now is largely limited to the paramilitary, security services, or armed forces tasked with winning and then delivering dwindling basics to society. Families are something you see—if you are lucky enough to have one—maybe once or twice a year.

Hope, truth, meaning—who has time for those things? And what were they anyways? What they result in—research, art, literature, science, discovery, creativity, knowledge—are all abandoned. What needless luxuries they now are. Every institution crumbles and is replaced by a perverse shadow of itself. It's of course easy for all this to seem distant and hard to grasp.

It all adds up, and you now realize you're spending more than three-quarters of your income just to (barely) stay alive. You know you're never going to get out of debt. There's a sense of degradation and desperation. All of this happens gradually, though it's already true for many even in the 2020s.

There are no trumpets, no announcements for the collapse of human society, the death of our humanity as we know it. It's the price of mass extinction. But you're not quite aware of it yet. You just know that you're bankrupt, and you barely survive on a line of credit. Without that credit, you and your family would starve in a matter of weeks or days.

1.13

DEEP DIVE INTO THE TRAGIC, PART 4: THE 2050s, THE FINAL GASPS

Now we conclude with the last decade, the 2050s, the shock of civilizational collapse with the second shock of existence on the horizon. Humanity's food chains have imploded. Water tables are poisoned with salt water. Raw materials are depleted or inaccessible, trapped behind curtains of flood and fire.

The very idea of there being a future—looking to tomorrow with any hope or possibility—is completely gone.

Shakespeare's line—"Tomorrow, and tomorrow, and tomorrow, creeps in this petty pace, day after day, to the last syllable of recorded time"—takes on new meaning as the second shock of existence seems to be a genuine possibility or likelihood. Indeed, tomorrow feels like "a tale told by an idiot, full of sound and fury, signifying nothing." **The last gasps of breath of a dying civilization are exhaled in a brutal battle for survival.**

The collapse of civilization—now a global civilization—unfolds just like every past local civilization, as Joseph Tainter points out in *The Collapse of Complex Societies*. For the first time, we have a global civilization operating on the same win-lose metrics, but now with exponential power capable of exponential destruction, and a tech plex that creates digital dictatorship run by TechnoFeudalism. The collapse of civilization is the collapse of the last shreds of the appearance of civility.

Remember the dystopia I referred to earlier, *Mad Max*—that's become reality. It's everyone for him or herself, with local bands coming together for brief alliances. *Mad Max* is made surreally manifest on a local and global scale simultaneously.

Neighbor turns on neighbor, ally turns on ally, society turns on itself. In the 2050s, the endgame of civilization begins in earnest. States declare independence, and the military is busy fighting wars, let's say, in the United States and in Canada for water, in Panama and in Iran for oil, in Europe for medicine, in China for food and labor—that's what the military is doing. Russia and China are now violent aggressors looking for resources to hoard. Family companies are dismantled and taken over by different Russian and Chinese interests. In Asia, China has brought its form of order to bear across the continent. The Belt and Road Initiative has now slowly, gradually turned into Chinese domination. By now, most of Asia and large parts of Africa are completely controlled by China. The cloak of deception in the form of benign intention is shed. Ethnocentric China, allied with Russia, now brutally rules in order to feed and clothe the elite of the world.

The current of fascist authoritarianism that had been gaining power in the 2040s now erupts into full view. By the 2050s, the shock of extinction, concentration camps, rampant abuse of immigrants, and local massacres are commonplace because who has energy to stop them in a world where the rivers are running dry and the oceans are turning to poison or dust? Of course, this is all intensified by artificial intelligence and machine learning, which may have by now completely replaced any form of human government.

Wasn't it only fair to blame all that misery on the other, on those dirty, filthy sub-humans? Who else could have caused it? In America, White Nationalism gains ascendance by offering a "promised land" to poor immigrants—but only those from White countries. In Great Britain, people continued blaming their problems on Europeans. In Europe, it was the Africans, the Jews, and the Muslims who were demonized. In India, it was all the non-Hindus. In China, everyone who wasn't of the Han majority.

We descend into an authoritarian techno-fascism, producing a world completely incapable of any genuine cooperation/coordination to solve the biggest problem of all: **the very collapse of civilization**. The macro systems and institutions break because there's no global coordination, because **there's no shared global intimacy, because global intimacy is based on a shared set of ordinating values**—none of those exist.

Everything breaks down, and it's at this point that the last of **the most crucial systems of humanity catastrophically, finally, and permanently fail**.

- Food chains implode.
- Water tables become salty.
- Medicine can no longer be made because the raw ingredients aren't accessible.
- There are no more elemental resources to be mined.
- Without a working ecosystem there's no insulin, there's no antibiotics.
- There's no milk, there's no eggs, there's no bread, there's no vegetables, there's no fruit,
- There's no computers, there's no cars, and there's no furniture.

All goods disappear because they simply can't exist without whole ecosystems to supply air, water, food, wood, metal. The resources we never even think about, and upon which our lives depend, are gone. The catastrophic trends from the 2040s continue, and by the 2050s ecosystems are poisoned, dead, inaccessible, or gone. The core stability of the oceans and their currents collapse. The seasons as we know them disappear.

A brutal and hostile world engulfs us.

Imagine America without the Mississippi river or India or Pakistan without the Ganges or other rivers fed by the Himalayan glaciers. Nations collapse. Despair and suicide are rampant. Traces of the impulse to survive drives people to violence, to fight for what's left. Towns turn on each other, larger countries fight wars, people are terrified or deadened into robotic monotony. **The ostensibly noble values of the postmodern liberal order—which said, "There *is* no real value"—are empty. Can you speak of freedom, goodness, and truth with anything but tired mockery?** Even the apparent aliveness of irony has disappeared.

Somewhere over these decades—or whatever time period it takes for each of these stages to unfold—the flourishing of civilization as we know it ends. The basic staples of food and medicine generated by the earth and all its ecosystems are gone. If you're still alive, whatever resources you have left are literally spent on bare survival.

At the same time, Google, Facebook, and Amazon are more powerful than ever. Their cadre of employees gets smaller and smaller—every year more and more are replaced by AI and machine learning. Those who remain, those who are absolutely necessary, are heavily protected in isolated pockets of physical beauty and safety. Of course, all three companies pay virtually no taxes, and governments have no funds available to prosecute them for violations anyway. The invisible primary systems collapse, and then all the secondary systems that depend on them collapse along with them. Children going to school need clean air, water, food, energy—all of which are in short supply by the 2030s and 2040s.

In the 2030s, your kids may have gone to school some days, but it's a charade, a place where they are just meant to be kept out of trouble for a while. If a school needs clean air, water, and food, and a hospital all the more so, where will they come from?

All those things are now gone. There are brownouts. Water stops flowing. The smog is so bad you can barely leave the house. You can go to the hospital, but just like school, it's a barely functioning, broken system. In the 2040s and 2050s, a bitter sense of disappointment permeates. Terrible new diseases break out every year or so.

It wasn't supposed to be this way.

You try and calm yourself after a moment of seeing red. If it still exists, you go into a virtual reality metaverse to try to calm yourself. You're smart enough to see the effects that living on the edge of despair has had on society. Massive waves of people seem to have lost their minds. They cling to bizarre superstitions, spending all their days in escapism, fleeing to the most absurd theories, joining Doomsday cults, or spending all day in VR worlds as **the memory of the future dies in our hearts, and global brutality takes over.**

The world is retribalized and brutal power rules.

Then sometime in the late 2050s, the whole thing collapses.

1.14

WHAT NEEDS TO HAPPEN: ARTICULATING A NEW STORY OF THE COSMOEROTIC UNIVERSE

Let's be clear: None of this needs to happen, but more or all of it will happen, unless something changes, gorgeously and beautifully—**and all of it absolutely can change if we move from this tragic perspective to the post-tragic.** We can step in, in the most beautiful way possible. We can move from despair to unimaginable joy. We can walk through this and become full human beings—according to the very intention of Cosmos itself.

Here's what needs to happen: Evolution needs to kick back in. It has moved to the background, and ecology took its place front and center. So we need evolution to kick back in. **We need to generate the next wave of evolution.** Are we ready to play a larger game? Are we ready to not bypass, to not just do great spiritual practice focused on our lives and basically ignore the world—are we ready to place attention, to *love*?

Love is not merely an emotion, love is a perception.

Love is the placing of attention—it's to be able to see.

The scenario that I just painted is certainly inaccurate in many ways. There are some people, like Tom, who are saying: by 2030 it's over. Then there are others, like David Attenborough, who think that this is going to take another sixty or seventy years for it to get really bad. There are many possibilities.

Regardless of the timeline, it's clear that evolution needs to kick back in. And for this to happen, it's not enough to say that exterior solutions are going to solve this. We've drained off the best data scientists in the world to work on optimizing Facebook's newsfeed, intensifying the hijacking of your attention, and increasing their quarterly profits. **Thousands of the best minds in the world that we would need for innovation are now simply hijacked by the tech plex.** And that's just one example among many.

We need to literally participate in the evolution of love, in the evolution of culture and consciousness. We need to evoke new social technologies based on new interior technologies. We can do it, without a doubt. It's fully possible through a deep da Vinci-like dive into the nature of Reality, into the universal story, into the story of human identity. We can articulate a new set of memes, a new story for a new humanity. We can change the source code.

We need to join genius to generate new memetic structures, just like democratization of governance emerged out of da Vinci and his cohort's formulations, in that time between worlds and time between stories, when the Renaissance generated the Western Enlightenment. **We need to move towards a new cultural enlightenment, which generates a new emergent, self-organized order—not a top-down order—in which the evolution of love transforms all of Reality.**

This is not fanciful conjecture.

Society begins to work together because we're moved by a new vision of value that's not just declared, but shown to be intrinsic.

Political will is only motivated by value or by the violation of value. When we saw George Floyd killed in Minneapolis, and everybody watched it, we saw the violation of value. Even in the middle of the pandemic while we were social distancing, this deep violation brought everyone into the streets, in the United States and all over the world, under the banner of Black Lives Matter. *There was a clear intrinsic value that we all shared.*

Only by aligning with value that is intrinsic to Reality, only by articulating a new story—the Intimate Universe, the Amorous Cosmos, the Cosmo-Erotic Universe, the fulfillment of *Homo sapiens* and *Homo amor*[6]—will we generate a political will that will reorganize Reality.

To do this, we'll address these questions in the chapters ahead:

- What do First Values mean, and what's in the way of their taking root?
- What does certainty mean, what does uncertainty mean?
- What are we sure about, and what are we unsure about?
- How do we live in this moment?
- How do we move from the tragic to the post-tragic?

It's absolutely ours to do—*and we can, we must, accomplish it with a joy that's unimaginable.*

---

[6] For a deeper dive on *Homo amor* and the Intimate Universe, see the forthcoming books, *The Intimate Universe, The Universe: A Love Story*, and *Homo Amor Manifesto*.

CHAPTER 2

FROM TRAGIC TO POST-TRAGIC: A VIEW OF WHAT IS POSSIBLE

THE VISION OF HOPE AND POSSIBILITY, AND WHY THE DOOMERS ARE WRONG

2.1

MOVING BEYOND POLARIZATION TOWARD A SHARED GRAMMAR OF VALUE

———————

Now we're moving into the second part of our journey, from the tragic to post-tragic. It would be a mistake to immediately say, "Oh, don't worry, there have been people talking about the end of the world since the beginning of time." Of course, there may be some validity to that, but it's just a defense, a way of closing down and truly avoiding the catastrophic and the tragic.

Seventy-five years after Bretton Woods, when we first interconnected the world in trade and technology, we're now facing a completely new landscape, characterized by extraction models, exponential growth curves, complicated and interrelated systems, and so many of the other issues we talked about yesterday, all of which are new. It's a socio-political landscape that's never existed before, which we must take seriously before responding to it; we are going to respond, and we are going to move from the tragic to the post-tragic.

The first crucial thing to understand is that the post-tragic transcends and includes the tragic. The post-tragic does not mean we revert to the

pre-tragic. In other words, if we do the denial move—the medication move, the ostrich's "bury my head in the sand" move, or the counter-attack move—we are regressing to the pre-tragic. We want to transcend and include the tragic into the post-tragic.

What's our poem from Yeats for the post-tragic?

> *When such as I cast out remorse,*
> *So great a sweetness fills my breast.*
> *We can dance, and we can sing.*
> *We are blest by everything.*
> *Everything we look upon is blest.*

When we cast out remorse, we come to this post-tragic level of consciousness. The key to the post-tragic level of consciousness is a deep and honest engagement with where we are, combined with a contemplation into the nature of Self, the nature of Reality, the nature of where we're coming from, and where we're going.

SILENCE OF ABSENCE AND SILENCE OF PRESENCE

There are two kinds of words, and two corresponding kinds of silence:

- There are words that come from speech, words that attempt to cover up uncertainty, discomfort, or the void, and our whole body resists those words; there's something violent about those words— they arise from the *silence of absence*.
- There are words that rise out of silence—not the silence of absence, but the *Silence of Presence*.

Even when Spirit seems silent, if I listen deeply and cultivate discernment, I can *know in my body with radical certainty* that that silence is fundamentally a Silence of Presence—a radical certainty that's not dogmatic. **It's not a certainty that stands in contradiction to uncertainty.**

So let's aim to speak words that come from the Silence of Presence.

Five-hundred years before the Common Era, one of the great lineage masters named this *chashmal*. This comes from what's called the account of the chariot, *ma'aseh merkavah*. In the interior sciences, the description of the enlightened state is *chash*, "silence," and *mal*, "words"—*words that arise from the silence*. So we offer a prayer that our words be poetry, because poetry arises from the silence, stretching, moving, finding form. Poetry is the movement of words that seek to break their boundary in limitation and stretch into the silence.

FROM CONTRADICTION TO PARADOX

The highest level of consciousness moves beyond polarization. We move from contradiction to paradox, where opposites dance as one—and the tantric principle of non-rejection is at play. So there's no contradiction between:

- Hope and hopelessness.
- Certainty and uncertainty.
- Silence and speech.

We hold both. Although we find cognitive expression, we also need a powerful noetic expression—expression in both traditional modes of knowledge and gnosis. **It's a deeper knowing, a carnal knowledge.** Adam *knew* his beloved Eve.

It's the knowledge of *Fuck*[7], of Eros. I know it in my body. Silence and speech dance together.

Let our silence and our speech be poetry.

There are many things that I'm radically uncertain about, and there are many things that I'm certain about, so certainty and uncertainty must dance together.

---

[7] By "Fuck," we mean our radical aliveness and the core nature of Reality. For a deeper dive, see "A Word on the Word Fuck," in *The Phenomenology of Eros, Volume One: From the Crisis of Desire to Sex Beyond Shame.*

WE NEED TO BE STRANGE ATTRACTORS

There's an enormous amount of bad thinking and bad feeling in the world. We mustn't move towards the lowest common denominator. We need to be a strange attractor. In systems theory, the strange attractor—even one that's just a minor fluctuation point, when the system is at disequilibrium— jumps the entire system to a higher level of order. We're at this moment of noetic change, of disequilibrium.

But in a moment like this, a minor fluctuation point, if it is articulated clearly—not because we're trained in speaking, not because we went viral on social media, not because we did good marketing, but in the way that people like Darwin, Freud, Leibniz, Kant, Ficino, da Vinci did—the content itself can be so self-evidently compelling that it changes the very fabric of Reality.

Of course, it's not that it doesn't need to be presented appropriately. It's not that we don't need the tools of marketing, nor all the instruments of this world of *samsara*, to bring *samsara* and nirvana together—we absolutely do. But we first need to pour all of ourselves into feeling and thinking clear-ly—and that's an effort. It can take tens of thousands of hours over decades, but we can also step into it right now.

If we can actually step out of the laziness of sloppy feeling and sloppy thinking, and take responsibility to become warriors, to become sense-makers, to be sensual —to be *sensual* is to engage in *sense-making*, even to the extent of familiarizing ourselves to know which sense-makers to trust—then we have the capacity to generate, beyond polarity, a shared universal grammar of value, which is non-totalitarian and not confined to just one religion.

It's not the removal of diversity. It's not the removal of conflict—conflict is wonderful, we absolutely need it. It's the removal of polarization. It's the realization that there's a common score of music that underlies all the instruments in the Unique Self Symphony.

I'll share a beautiful image. There were two great American politicians, complex figures, both of them, that I'm sure everyone's heard of: John F. Kennedy and Richard Nixon. Each of those names evokes a very different response, and we have a different sense in our body for each. They fought bitterly against each other in the presidential election of 1960. But actually, Kennedy and Nixon were good friends. They became friends in 1947, sharing a bunk and staying up all night talking and drinking as they were taking a train to Washington, and remained close throughout the 1950s. Underneath their very different positions, there was *a Shared Grammar of Value*. They didn't know quite how to articulate it. It was assumed to them. They didn't put a lot of time into articulating it; it was just a given.

That shared grammar of value has been increasingly deconstructed around the world in the decades since, as we've moved through the postmodern intervention in Reality, which has aimed to deconstruct all value, and says there is no intrinsic value in Cosmos.

So what we need to do together is fully engage in this radically amazing, wondrous, gorgeous *reconstructive project*, where we can begin to see the way to a shared Universal Grammar of Value. That's our context.

2.2

THE FIRST STEPS FROM TRAGIC TO POST-TRAGIC: FINDING LOVE IN A HOPELESS PLACE

It's important to note that the specter of the death of humanity, which we already looked at in brutal detail, is no greater challenge to meaning and love than the unjust suffering and death of a single human being. That's an incredibly important sentence that's critical to understand. The notion that I shrink away and hide in the face of the death of humanity and not in the face of the death of a single human being, is fundamentally wrong from a feeling perspective, from an epistemological perspective, and from a thinking perspective. It fundamentally misunderstands Reality.

The death of an individual human being, if you understand the infinite irreducible dignity of everyone, is no less a challenge than the death of humanity. It's impossible to understand Reality as being Good, True, and Beautiful if we understand Reality as exhausting itself in one dimension. By one dimension, I mean physical life on earth as we know it. **Anyone who suggests that Reality exhausts itself in one dimension, and is also filled with intrinsic value, goodness, truth, and beauty, is almost definitely a narcissist.** For example, someone who says, "Well, things are pretty bad, but my life's okay. I wasn't in Rwanda, I couldn't do anything. So I'll just read philosophy, and it will all work out."

Again: The death of humanity is not a greater challenge to love, and to value, and to intrinsic meaning, than the death and unjust suffering of one individual human being. This is critical to understand.

Some of those who are having Doomer conversations are beautiful people, living in beautiful, modern and postmodern privilege, who realize that all this just might affect them sooner than later. Well, these trends and influences have been affecting people for millennia. Any attempt to use theology or spirituality—whether it's New Age spirituality or classical theology—to deaden our sensitivity to pain, is not kosher. The false certainties that try to "explain" suffering need to be thrown out. *There is no certainty, no rationale, no explanation that stands in the face of burning children.*

EITHER EVERYTHING IS MEANINGFUL OR NOTHING IS

At the same time, there's an enormous amount of information—and not just radical empirical information of the kind that was starting to be gathered by the Cambridge Society with Sidgwick, and William James at the Harvard Psychical Research Society, but information that lives in our bodies—confirming that the world is intrinsically valuable.

We understand that everything is meaningful or nothing's meaningful, and the notion that nothing is meaningful, we know in our very bodies and cells every single day, to be untrue.

It matters greatly whether we love each other or not.

It matters whether I plunge a knife into you or we embrace.

Similarly, we can't engage Reality from the perspective of only one life-time—that's impossible. Justice, fairness, and the fullness of meaning aren't exhausted in a single lifetime. There's a wide range of empirical information available from the interior sciences that points to a multi-dimensional Reality. **The radical empiricism of the interior sciences is accessed through the Eye of the Heart, which is intrinsically, anthro-ontologically available to every human being**.

Most materialists and those under the sway of the postmodern story think this world is the end of the story, that matter triumphs, and that meaning is ultimately an illusion. As such, the potential death of humanity—or the death of most of humanity until there's a regeneration, which is really what the Doomers are talking about, after which the cycle starts again—is a moment that would end everything.

But, in fact, I understand that we live in a world in which meaning cannot be understood to be filled coherently within one dimension—the physical, material world—in the course of one lifetime. This is true in all the horrific tragedies of history, for the children slaughtered in Rwanda, or those who died in gas chambers during the Holocaust—I'm talking about my immediate family, including aunts, grandparents, the whole gang. It's important to understand.

The potential death of humanity, or most of humanity, would obviously be a horrific tragedy, if that's the way Reality goes. But I don't believe there's any reason Reality *has* to go that way; we can stand at the pivot point, and be the Universe in person.

We're not in the Universe—we are the Universe, and we are the voice of the Universe. The Universe lives and moves in us, as us, and through us.

It's inaccurate to take ourselves out of the equation and say the Universe is going to *do* something. Clearly, the way the Universe moves is the way we move, because the most accurate understanding of self-identity is that *I am, each of us is, the Universe in person.* The notion that the Universe is going to do something apart from us is absurd. There is no separation.

UNIQUE SELF AND FORGIVENESS

One way to grasp this notion that we can't hold it all within the cycle of just one lifetime is through the notion of forgiveness. This sentence from Mark Twain is unimaginable, and so beautiful:

"Forgiveness is the fragrance that the violet sheds to the heel that crushed it."

This is an impossible sentence to grasp within the frame of a small separate-self human being who hasn't accessed the deeper interior science of True Self, who hasn't accessed the deeper interior science of Unique Self, of *Homo sapiens* fulfilled as *Homo amor.*

Within the frame of one lifetime—and certainly within the frame of rivalrous, separate self, zero-sum conflict governed by win-lose metrics, a narrow success story governed by status, material success, accumulation, and limited separate self productivity—true forgiveness is a total impossibility.

In our lives, we've all been betrayed at some point—in some sense we've all been Jesus, and in some sense we've all been Judas. *You can only be betrayed by someone who would never betray you, because that's the nature of betrayal.*

The technology of forgiveness is not the mere release of accountability, since the person is still accountable, and it's not the turning of the other cheek that distorts Reality. Rather, the notion that I can release the hatred and begin again requires that I step out of the narrowness of one dimension, one lifetime, and feel into a larger field. That's what True Self means, or what William James called "wider self." I move from separate self to True Self through contemplation or meditation or breathwork or prayer or ecstatic dance or lovemaking, or other means—I'm blown away and merged into nature. **When I step into the fullness of True Self, I step out of the narrowness of the ego story into something much wider.**

True Self itself is another dimension, beneath the space-time continuum, which is the next unfolding after separate self, in a multi-dimensional and interdimensional Reality. **You can't even begin to access forgiveness without blowing your heart open and accessing this wider and deeper level of Reality.**

ETTY HILLESUM TALKING TO THE SECOND FACE OF SPIRIT

I mentioned the Holocaust because it's a key frame of reference in my life. I want to introduce you to Etty Hillesum, who wrote a diary at the time. Hillesum was a robust, tormented, and sensual woman, liberated into her full feminine intersexuality, into her mind and her heart, who lived in the thriving metropolis of Amsterdam before the war. As the Nazis continued their campaign of genocide, her future became more and more uncertain, and she began to find ways of addressing the Divine directly. She didn't live in a religious context, but she found her way to these direct sacred conversations, intuitively understanding that Divinity or Spirit is not only the Infinity of Power, but what we've called the Infinity of Intimacy.

She clearly saw that the Infinity of Power and the Infinity of Intimacy are, in some sense, inseparable. She honored and loved the power, and honored and loved the intimacy. She had this strange set of conversations with the Divine. And she was writing when she'd already been taken into the depths of despair, already knowing that she's not going to get out of this life alive—and that the depth of the individual human being is unfathomable.

She turns to what we call in our language, the second face of Reality, the personhood of Reality, the Second Face of Spirit:

- She's talking to God.
- She's talking to Source.
- She's talking to Spirit.
- She's talking to Geist.
- She's talking to the Implicate Order.
- She's talking to the Atman that's Brahman.
- She's talking to the Eros of Cosmos.

Because there are only two choices in our lives: **either Reality is the result of an *oops*, complete randomness, or Reality is an emergent of an intentional movement of Cosmos.**

Even in the beginnings of science, it's very clear: there are only sixteen kinds of quark among the gazillions that comprise Reality in the first nanoseconds after the Big Bang. But why sixteen? If you step out of the dogmas of scientism and into true science, as more and more are beginning to do at the leading edge, you realize that **there's an essential, non-random direction in Reality**, which is stunning beyond imagination.

As she's facing death, Hillesum is speaking to this Personhood of Cosmos. Here's what she says, and it's literally a sacred text:

> *Alas, there doesn't seem to be much You Yourself can do about our circumstances, about our lives. Neither do I hold You responsible. You cannot help us, but we must help You and defend Your dwelling place inside us to the last.*[8]

---

[8] Etty Hillesum, Diary Entry, 12 July 1942. The full quotation reads: "These are scary times, my God. Tonight was the first time that I lay sleepless in the dark with burning eyes and many images of human suffering passed me by. I'll promise you one thing, God, just one little thing: I won't hang my worries about the future like so many heavy weights on the present day, but that takes a certain amount of practice. Every day is now enough for itself. I'll help you God, that you don't break down in me, but I can't vouch for anything in advance. But this one thing is becoming more and more clear to me: that you cannot help us, but that we must help you and through the latter we help ourselves. And this is the only thing we can save in this time and also the only thing that matters: a piece of you in ourselves, God. And maybe we too can help dig you up in the ravaged hearts of others. Yes, my God, you don't seem to be able to do too much about circumstances, they are also part of this life. I won't hold you accountable for it either, you can hold us accountable for it later. And almost with

That's the beginning of the movement from the tragic to the post-tragic. Was she right that we cannot hold Divinity responsible? There's a whole tradition of masters who put God on trial, so let's leave that aside for a moment. But what she clearly understood was several of the main First Principles of Cosmos:

- There is revelation and there's mystery.
- There is certainty and there's uncertainty.
- There is the voice that speaks and there's the silence.

There are dramatic moments throughout history in which Reality is shrouded in mystery, and in those moments, the voice of Spirit, the voice of love, and the voice of meaning live and breathe in us. We become not the entire story, but one face of Spirit in person. It's in those moments, founded not in the silence of absence but in the Silence of Presence, when we understand that this dimension cannot exhaust all of Reality:

- We don't turn to despair—we don't give up hope.
- *We are hope itself*—we incarnate hope.
- We are Divinity in person.
- We are the language of the Divine.
- We're God's verbs, we're God's adjectives, we're God's nouns, and God's dangling modifiers.

We know that in those moments, at least within the limited frame of the space-time continuum in this dimension, God may not always help us in the way that we would like, but that **we must help God**; we must assure with every fiber of our being, that we protect Her dwelling place inside us.

And then *we can cast out remorse,* and *everything we look upon is blest.*

At every stage, we're going to find a new level of hope. So we started in a hopeless place in chapter one, and now we're beginning to find love again.

---

every heartbeat it becomes clearer to me: that you cannot help us, but that we must help you and that we must defend to the last the house within us where you live."

In response to the tragic, we need to fully come alive and *find love in a hopeless place*. That's what Etty Hillesum does. She's in the kingdom of the night, and she finds love in a hopeless place. When we forgive in the kingdom of the night, we find love in a hopeless place. Then we realize that the Universe is not happening *to* us, but that the Universe actually lives *in* us, that we ourselves inhabit and contribute to a participatory Cosmos—and **in a participatory Cosmos there's room for heroes**.

Heroes are the early adopters of *Homo amor*, and heroes are not just individuals. Sixty or seventy years ago, a bunch of Jewish kids in Cleveland started writing comic books, and they called them *Superman*—the one hero, the one Messiah. Now we understand that it's not about any one single Unique Self, but rather about a Unique Self Symphony, a group of empowered individuals acting in concert together. So now we have the entire Marvel Universe of superheroes working together. That's a good start, but we need to move beyond that, to a Democratization of Enlightenment, where we all become heroes.

We invoke this new collective intelligence, and we begin, as Rihanna's song says, to *find love in a hopeless place*.[9]

---

[9] Listen to "We Found Love" by Rihanna ft. Calvin Harris, to get a taste of hope.

2.3

THE STORY OF ARMAGEDDON IN THE GREAT TRADITIONS

The Doomer notion that we are inevitably running into potential catastrophic scenarios where the world explodes or life dies out entirely is not a new idea. We've all heard of Armageddon. There's a version of it in Christianity, another in Buddhism, several major versions of it in Hinduism, and others in the Native American traditions. There are different names for it in every great tradition, and there's no tradition in the world that doesn't have a notion that at a certain moment in history, **there's a crossroads where things could either open up (Messiah) or end in tragedy (Armageddon).** Different traditions had this realization, which they got from deep contemplation in the interior sciences, that time in the human world doesn't go on inexorably, forever the way it is, but that there's actually a movement whereby things transform.

However, the great religions hijacked this intuition in an ethnocentric way. All the great traditions had a deep, transcultural, and transtemporal realization that we'll arrive at a pivot point—but they said that "everyone's either going to realize that *our* religion is true and they convert, or they're going to burn in hell." All of this was the realization of the interior sciences before the insights of evolution had been theorized. They understood the possibility of Armageddon as happening through a combination of socio-political events and spiritual events, but obviously, there was no exponential technology—no post-nuclear exponential technology diffused among non-state actors—and most of the existential risks we now face were not a threat.

Yet, the interior technologies described not just the collapse of an individual civilization, but the collapse of civilization itself. Thus, there's a sense in interior science of a moment in time in which, as Robert Frost puts it, "two roads diverge in a wood." And either we step up and take our seat at the table of history, or we move towards some sort of implosion. That's one of the oldest ideas in humanity.

We turned our attention away from it for a while, and now we see a particular devastating expression of this idea looming before us, animated by an existential risk landscape we've never seen before. But the fundamental idea has always been there.

The only reason we dismissed the idea, somewhat skillfully and understandably, is that it was hijacked in an ethnocentric way. It was ascribed to a God who was only in the sky and not on earth, who chose only one people, who damned everyone else, and who would punish those who didn't obey his strictures against petty ritual infractions and self-pleasuring. **In other words, there was a good reason for rejecting that, so it was rejected. But we threw the baby out with the bathwater—we forgot that this intuition about Messiah and Armageddon has something important, even vital, to say.**

I remember reading a third-century text when I was nineteen years old, in *Tractate Sanhedrin*. There are two words in the text that repeat again and again: *be'ita achishena*, which means history will triumph in a new way in its right time, and there will be an opening to new possibilities. It's like the dawning of the Age of Aquarius: "When the Moon's in the seventh house, and Jupiter aligns with Mars." But that's just a way of saying that there's this potential dawning of a new humanity. We're now in what we call the Anthropocene, where the human being can participate in creating that possibility. We call that Messianism, which is not about some dude or dudette riding on a white donkey into Jerusalem. ***It's about the possibility of a new era dawning.***

This too was hijacked, but the intuition remains profound, and it's a critical intuition that needs to be understood, because it opens up the door to the emergence of *Homo amor.*

2.4

APPROPRIATE PRAISE
FOR MODERNITY

In the conversation between Tom and Jack cited in the last chapter, you might have noticed an underlying dismissal of modernity, which is considered evil in some sense because of where we've ended up. That's a huge mistake that we need to begin disabusing ourselves of.

Just a couple hundred years ago, there were half a billion people in the world, and now today there are close to eight billion—an intense explosion of beautiful life. Every single one of those eight billion people has a unique quality of intimacy, and is an irreducibly unique expression of Reality that is:

- Filled with wonder.
- Filled with capacity.
- Filled with perception.
- Filled with qualia.
- Filled with colors and sounds and wonder and delight.
- Filled with the potential to make love, touch, be filled with quivering tenderness and the fierceness of delight, to experience poignancy and potency, and transmute pain into art.

There are 7.5 billion new expressions of unique intimacy and life, and modernity helped enable all this beauty and joy and wonder. Of course, we need to be appropriately critical of modernity, but the institution we call science is—not exclusively, but in large part—responsible for all this. It's a new way of thinking about the Cosmos, a new way of organizing and understanding Reality, and it deserves appropriate praise.

DISCONTINUITY AND CONTINUITY BETWEEN HUMANS AND THE WORLD

It is certainly true that Newton and Descartes didn't understand many important things about animals. Descartes thought they were essentially like machines, and for all intents and purposes basically didn't exist. There were older great traditions, like the Biblical tradition, that had prohibitions against inflicting any kind of pain to animals, but there was also a kind of brutality towards animals in many of the great traditions. Modernity spoke sharply into the discontinuity between human beings and the rest of the world. This is true in part—of course, there are important distinctions between human beings and the rest of the world—but there's also a deep continuity. **Animals and humans exist in an ongoing, unfolding dialectic of continuity and discontinuity**.

In some sense, the continuity is clear. The notion that there are dancing allurements of protons and electrons, and that that's the beginning of the movement of Eros in Cosmos, is unbelievably important and has enormous implications—and it extends to all levels of Reality. Having said that, the discontinuities are very clear as well. How many of you have ever dated a rock? Plants are filled with allurement, but how many people have dated a plant? How many people here have dated a cat? Let's get real.

Of course, we can commune with all forms of nature. We can talk about the continuity between rocks, trees, and cats, but let's not lose sight of the important discontinuities. Here's where the New Age gets in trouble. Of course there's continuity, but first, let's own the discontinuity: **Rocks,** plants, and cats don't build hospitals for people who are vulnerable. It doesn't happen. They also don't create nuclear weapons. And so, there's an obvious discontinuity between human beings and the rest of the world, while there's also an obvious continuity.

Twenty years ago, in *Psychology Today*, there was an article about eight dimensions of Reality that exist only in the human world, things like play and humor. In the last twenty years of research, we've seen that there are ancient expressions of virtually all these dimensions in the mammalian world. So of course, we can have deep, even profound interconnections with the world of matter and the world of plants and animals.

There's a profound continuity between humans and non-humans that we lost; and there are important discontinuities—they're both true.

Some parts of society emphasize the continuity and lose sight of the obvious and important discontinuity. There's a real movement from Bacteria to Bach, a real movement from Slime to Shakespeare, a real movement from Mud to Mozart. The human being is, in some unique sense, *Homo Imago Dei*: a unique incarnation; the human being *does* awaken as conscious evolution.

At the moment when modernity emerged, we emphasized the discontinuity and lost the continuity. This didn't happen because Descartes was evil, but because he was ignorant; he didn't understand. Descartes and others who reawakened of a sense of universals were still locked in their own worldviews:

- They had egocentric love: they had a felt sense of care and concern for their family and their people.
- They had ethnocentric love: they could expand the love to cover their whole religion or their whole nation.

But since then, many segments of society have moved into worldcentric intimacy, or worldcentric love (I don't call it "world-centric consciousness"). Meaning: the realization of sharing an identity with every human being on the planet.

We need to evolve love, and the evolution of love is the expansion of the boundaries of love.

But we can move even beyond worldcentric intimacy. Lots of people still eat steaks and hamburgers because we're locked at worldcentric and haven't gotten to **cosmocentric intimacy: the felt sense of shared identity and mutuality of pathos and recognition with all animals and plants, with a much wider field, and ultimately with Gaia itself and then beyond Gaia, into the wild Cosmos, into the Universe.**

Of course there's an evolution of love. Having said that, we can't demonize modernity, since it exploded and expanded Reality in many ways. Seven and a half billion new Unique Selves live at this moment in time because of modernity. Universal human rights don't come from indigenous societies living at the Dunbar number of 150. So let's be careful of this retro-romantic fallacy.

MODERNITY *IS* BEAUTIFUL

Steven Pinker is not entirely wrong, though he's definitely not entirely right, in his praise of modernity and the Western Enlightenment tradition, which includes:

- The emergence of the feminine.
- The emergence of universal human rights.
- The emergence of new modes and evolutions of goodness.
- The move from ethnocentric to worldcentric intimacy.
- The evolution of truth through the emergence of science.

The emergence of science is not just the evolution of truth, it's also the evolution of beauty: to enter into the dazzling microscopic world of a cell, to understand the interior of the human body, to feel into the tectonic plates that move the Earth, to begin to understand the laws of motion with Kepler and Galileo, to understand classical physics with Newton, and then into the quantum world, to understand a flower in a way that we never could 200 years ago. **These are dazzling revelations, not just of truth, but also of beauty—and all of this takes place in modernity.**

But here's where it gets a little confusing: the sheer amount of pain and suffering in the world has also dramatically increased in the modern period. There are currently about two billion people in the world without adequate drinking water, challenged with "food insecurity," experiencing starvation, nutritional depletion, contaminated drinking water, disease... the list goes on. This is what Steven Pinker forgets to tell you. If there were half billion people on the planet a couple hundred years ago, and not all of them are suffering, and there's eight billion today, of which there's perhaps two billion suffering, that means we've virtually quadrupled the amount of suffering. The sheer amount of pain and suffering in the world has dramatically increased—and we often forget that.

Modernity is complex—*it has such great dignities and such great disasters.* The sense of depression and malaise, as well as obesity, suicide, opioid addiction, and mental breakdown, are at play in a significant portion of the contemporary population. But that doesn't in any way disqualify the great dignities of modernity.

THE APOCALYPTIC VIEW MISSES THE BASIC MOVEMENT OF EVOLUTION ITSELF

Richard Branson and Jeff Bezos both recently went to space. What began the space race? What takes a rocket ship into space? It's not mere fuel, but human spirit. John F. Kennedy, in that great speech he gave some sixty years ago, spoke about reaching for the next frontier, and he spoke of possibility. Our capacity to step into space, to reach for outer space, and our equal capacity to reach for inner space are both equally important, and we need to do them together. They're both animated by the opposite of the Doomer grief:

They're animated by *hope.*

They're animated by the *human spirit.*

They're animated by the *evolutionary impulse.*

Getting rockets into outer space is one potential response to existential risk. But we can also plunge into inner space and generate new interior technologies, generate a new collective intelligence, generate a new Grammar of Value that actually awakens as Unique Self Symphonies all over the world.

This is the groundswell movement of consciousness—not top-down command and control, but the self-organizing Universe—moving with a new shared intelligence. That's what happened in Athens, Alexandria, and in the Renaissance.

Whenever there's a new collective intelligence that explodes into a genuine new vision of the world, based on the best available empirical facts—in both the interior and exterior sciences—we literally change the course of history. If we only look away or behind us, we get stuck in the pre-tragic. If we only look down at what's immediately happening, we remain in the tragic, and it becomes a self-perpetuating tragedy.

We need to honor and move through both of these perspectives, but in order to shift into the post-tragic, we've got to look up, look ahead, *and* look inwards. We've got to look up to outer space, and we've got to look inside and be animated by the very nature of the evolutionary impulse itself that lives within each one of us.

2.5

REALITY IS NOT JUST A FACT—REALITY IS A STORY

Most religions, in the most general possible terms, have historically viewed this world as a mere hallway to the next world. In other words, this world or this dimension is not central. Here we're tested and we're tried in this crucible of soul-making, and then we move to the next world. That was religion's basic move, historically speaking.

This idea has had great value, but it was also a tragic limitation. Although there are many beautiful qualities of the religious perspective, we need to move beyond the traditional forms, with their many shadows. Besides all the corruptions of religion, it has a tendency to strip the world of its dignity; **it tends to strip away the intrinsic value of this world**. But Reality itself generates value; Reality is filled with value. And what religions often did was to devalue Reality.

Now, let's talk about science. Just as this view does not include *all* of religion, what I'm about to say about science is not *all* of science. There are many other voices in science today, but I'm talking about a kind of *orthodox scientism.* For at least a few hundred years, Reality itself was viewed as inert. Most scientists were either materialists or dualists, believing this world is dead, lifeless, and governed by precise mechanical laws, and that "to know something" is to take it apart and reduce it to its most essential dimensions—its subatomic particles, for example. That's how you know Reality. There's a true and real sense of a mechanical world governed by immutable mechanical laws, but this materialist or dualist notion ultimately devalues Reality, because it doesn't understand it.

So let's get this clear. **Both religion in its fundamentalist shadow forms, and scientism in its fundamentalist, dogmatic materialist forms, devalued Reality.**

But there's a third view of Reality that's becoming increasingly current, at least at the leading edges of some of the best writing today in the world. Alfred North Whitehead, who wrote *Principia Mathematica* with Bertrand Russell, is one of the key precursors in this conversation, as was Teilhard de Chardin, Charles Sanders Peirce, James Mark Baldwin, and others. This is a different and a deeper understanding, and critically important in the interior sciences—if you know where to find it. Kropotkin was also one of the key figures, that great Russian prince who offers an alternative lineage to Darwin that's now being adopted in the mainstream of the Academy by prominent evolutionary scientists like David Sloan Wilson.

THE FIRST THREE BIG BANGS

We can track this in the notion of what we might call the three Big Bangs. I don't want to call this religion or science, but rather it follows from the evolutionary notion that *Reality is not just a fact, Reality is a story.* **Reality is going somewhere. There's a non-random *telos* in Cosmos.** Science correctly had an allergy to *telos* because it was identified with premodern religion, which hijacked this conception in the most cruel and corrupt ways. But once you get beyond that hijacking, you begin to realize that Reality *is* going someplace, just not in the way we once thought, according to religion. It's developing from quarks to life to human culture—and beyond.

There is a clear movement in that direction, **a gradual deepening and expansion of ever greater layers of depth**, and you can understand this story through the three Big Bangs.

1. **The First Big Bang is the explosion of matter.** When matter explodes, it goes through all these stages of development: from the sixteen kinds of basic quarks, to trios of quarks that combine into protons and neutrons 380,000 years later. There's an allurement between protons and electrons, and atoms are formed, followed by molecules and more complex configurations of the physical world. This allurement drives Reality—this Eros animates the four forces of Cosmos in what we can refer to as the "Telerotic Universe." So we progressively move through the world of matter until the next major shift.

2. **The Second Big Bang is the explosion of life from matter.** The way we might say it is that matter *triumphs* into life. Life doesn't *exclude* matter—life *loves* matter. Life includes matter in its embrace. Life is built on the embrace of matter. Life then evolves, life deepens; intimacies intensify. So we move through stages of life: from amoeba to fungus to plant to amphibian, and then vertebrate life, early animals and later animals. Then we get to mammals and then early hominids walking on the savanna. This is not the movement of the physiosphere, but the biosphere. It's the triumph of the physiosphere in the biosphere; the triumph of matter in life.

3 **The Third Big Bang is the emergence of the self-reflective human mind.** This generates language, and culture, and an ability to be self-conscious. It takes time; it goes through many stages of development. Jean Gebser outlines five of them, while others outline twelve, or seventeen. But basically, there's a clear understanding that Reality develops and unfolds through structure-stages. One way that we

characterize this development is through the progressive unfolding of wider forms of intimacy:

- From **egocentric** intimacy in individuals, families, and clan,
- To **ethnocentric** intimacy in the tribes and empires,
- To **worldcentric** intimacy, following the Western Enlightenment,
- To the beginning of a movement, currently at the leading edge, of **cosmocentric** intimacy, where we realize that we're an expression of the Universe itself—not only do *we live in the Intimate Universe, but the Intimate Universe lives in us.*

So, the Third Big Bang is the emergence of the self-reflective human mind. Life triumphs in a new form and a new quality of life; life that generates Proust and Shakespeare and self-reflection and heroism, the building of hospitals, and care for the most vulnerable. That's the human, self-reflective mind, **the triumph of the biosphere in the noosphere**, the Third Big Bang.

So does it just end then? Do we just plateau? Do we now just start to wind it all down? No, that's absurd! The movement of Reality is non-random, and Reality moves towards ever ascending structures of consciousness.

What is the triumph of the Third Big Bang in the narrative arc of Cosmos? What is the new emergence? Where do we move from human life? This is the beginning of the new story, what we're calling the Fourth Big Bang.

A NEW POSSIBILITY: THE FOURTH BIG BANG

The Fourth Big Bang is the triumph of *Homo sapiens* as *Homo amor*. **It's the realization that I don't just live in a Universe, but in an *Intimate Universe*—and it's the realization that the Intimate Universe lives in, as, and through me.**

- True Self is not just my identity with the field of consciousness.
- True Self itself is the realization that nothing exists independently from anything else.

93

- True Self itself is the realization of the radical interconnectivity—and the interior of interconnectivity is intimacy, *the radical, intimate interconnectivity of the All with the All.*

But we don't stop there. We then realize that the Universe—which is not dead or inert, but animated by Eros—is within me, that I am an emergence, and what lives in me is all the muons and hadrons, all the protons and electrons, all the atoms, all the macromolecules, all the cells, all the multicellular structures, and all the structures since the First Big Bang.

Evolution is trustable because it never forgets a breakthrough—all breakthroughs are held by evolution. **All of matter, all of life, and all of the human self-reflective mind, lives in us.** Then this Fourth Big Bang explodes, in either the Doomer scenario of Armageddon, or in *Homo amor*, in a new possibility—the Possibility of Possibility.

THE TRIUMPH OF HOMO SAPIENS AS HOMO AMOR

The Fourth Big Bang is not a fanciful conjecture, blind hubris, or a delusion of grandeur —and that's why we can align with it. **The Fourth Big Bang is the inherent evolutionary movement in the logic of Cosmos itself.** That's what all the great traditions understood.

Now, when they talked about this, they sometimes called it Messiah or Buddha, but they exiled Messiah to one person or nation, or they exiled Buddha to the enlightened ones or individual avatars. All of those had an important role to play historically, and all of those were and will continue to be important. But we need to move beyond the singular Buddha, to the Sangha of Buddhas. **The next Buddha is not only a Sangha, it's also a collection of Buddhas acting in concert together. The community itself needs to become a Unique Self Symphony, the new structure of the evolution of intimacy.**

This is a new evolutionary intimacy, a new structure of Eros, which is the generative movement of Cosmos.

WE ARE THE VOICE OF THE FUTURE, WE DESIRE THE FUTURE

If we get lost in being present and living in love right now—but abandoning hope—we completely betray the future:

+ We betray *Homo amor.*
+ We betray the evolutionary impulse.
+ We betray God.
+ We betray She.
+ We betray the Possibility of Possibility that lives alive and awake in us.
+ We betray the future—when we're the future's only voice.
+ We betray the covenant between generations.

We are the voice of the future. There is a covenant between generations, and we need to embrace the "memory of the future" that lives in us. That's what it means to find love in a hopeless place. That's what it means to create a space program, to go to outer space. That's also what it means to go to inner space and find the truth within. That's what it means to look up and not look down—not to stay stuck in the present tragedy.

A kind of apocalyptic thinking which says "let's focus all the attention on this generation of doom"—which closes itself off to the radical, incessant, ceaseless creativity of Cosmos that lives awake and alive in us—is the ultimate abandonment of our very humanity. It's that which allows the indwelling Divine to die in us. **The Fourth Big Bang is the triumph of the separate self *Homo sapiens* into True Self, into the realization that**

95

I'm one with the field of consciousness. But it's also a deepening of True Self itself. I realize I'm not just one with the field of consciousness—I'm one with the field of consciousness *and desire*. Reality is desire, and desire always reaches for the future. That's the nature of desire—"I desire the future." This is shocking and beautiful beyond belief.

I'm desiring the future, a much better future. That desire for a Reality which is beyond racism, for a Reality in which *every* human being on the face of the planet awakens and knows that they are an irreducible Unique Self, where their gifts are honored, and their story deserves to be lived and told. That's *Homo amor*: We come to know that we're each of us the personal face of the evolutionary impulse, that Reality actually *needs* our service, and that our lives are inherently dignified. That's a genuine possibility for every human being on the planet.

CLAIMING OUR DESTINY AS THE GREATEST PIONEERS

Modernity got a lot of it wrong: it got lost in separate self, and it over-valued the material world. But it deeply contributed to the ground of this possibility, just like matter gives us the ground of life, and life gives us the ground of self-reflective mind. ***Homo sapiens*' self-reflective mind needs to not be castigated and made evil—it's not evil. It's just sometimes ignorant, lost in shadow.** We need to recognize the shadow and move through it and move through the void, and claim our destiny as the greatest pioneers in human history of both inner and outer space.

That means we need to move beyond the individual avatar of Spirit and into Unique Self Symphony, to move towards a new emergent order, a new cultural enlightenment, a new collective intelligence, in which **the Universe self-organizes into Unique Self Symphonies that have the capacity to release an exponential level of creativity and power, unlike that which has ever been seen before.**

2.6

MOVING TO COSMOCENTRIC INTIMACY

In the late 1960s, a group of serious people were talking a lot about starvation. The Club of Rome published a book called *The Limits of Growth*, and William Paddock and Paul Ehrlich wrote another major book called *The Population Bomb*. There was a widespread notion that we were going to basically run out of food, and we'd have a worldwide famine and starvation. By now, according to them, famine and starvation were supposed to have swept through the world entirely.

But it didn't happen. While Ehrlich was writing that, "the battle to feed humanity has already been lost," it was in fact being vigorously fought. In Mexico, in the late 1950s and early 1960s, a young plant scientist named Norman Borlaug led an effort, funded by the Mexican government and the Rockefeller Foundation, to develop new strains of wheat that can be planted more often, that would produce more and bigger seeds, and that could resist common diseases. The results in Mexico were outstanding. Borlaug's wheat varieties produced three times as much grain as conventional breeds, and by 1963, more than ninety percent of Mexico's wheat crop was planted using Borlaug's seeds. The total wheat harvest was an astounding six times what it had been in 1944, the year Borlaug started his work. Mexico was then more than self-sufficient in wheat and soon became a wheat exporter.

By 1967, Borlaug's new wheat varieties were being planted around the world, which greatly helped stave off forecasted famines in India, Pakistan, and Turkey. Three years later, in 1970, the Nobel Committee awarded the unassuming, pickup-driving Borlaug the Nobel Peace Prize, for his efforts that had saved the lives of billions.

Now, had Borlaug been looking back or down and not looking up or ahead, what would he have done? How tragic would it have been if he had gone to an old version of True Self and meditated his way away, working on dissolving his pain body? How tragic would it have been if Borlaug had decided he was a post-Doomer, and just been fully present with life, beautifully, every day, waiting for the imminent, inevitable doom?

Fuck that! That's a violation of value. And in fact, we've got to do both. We look in all directions, backwards and forwards, upwards and down, right here where we are. We've got to generate both exterior technologies and interior technologies.

Similarly, the tragic mistake of books like *The Infinite Resource,* by Ramez Naam, is that they think that innovation will happen by itself. They fail to understand that innovation is an expression of a Universe story based on intrinsic value. When Borlaug was innovating in the late 1950s and early 1960s, he was motivated by his enormous sense of value, and a refusal to accept the predictions of certain, near-term doom predicted by Paul Ehrlich and others. Borlaug's work was deeply flawed, as we shall see, but his profound belief in the value of solving world hunger was a lifesaver for millions. That sense of value has been deconstructed in a profound way **and we need to reconstruct it again in order to align with, and become, the intrinsic value of Cosmos itself.**

We need to understand why that apocalyptic notion—the sense that there's this inexorable Armageddon fast approaching—is hugely mistaken, and misses the basic movement of evolution itself. It doesn't mean that there isn't a *possibility* that we will not take responsibility for Reality—we are evolution in person. **But there is *a radical optimism* in the structure of evolution**, and it's critical that we animate this again.

• • •

Here is a text from Abraham Kook, an evolutionary mystic, a proto-*Homo amor*, who doesn't yet have the exact language, but who gets close. He speaks to this exact issue of evolution: "More than all other philosophical teachings, the doctrine of evolution"—and he's talking here about scientific evolution, and the *interior* implications of evolution—"that's currently conquering the world adopts well, is aligned with, the inner science of interior wisdom. Evolution, which advances in the direction of betterment, provides the optimistic essence of the world. For how can one despair when one sees that everything is unfolding and improving?"

We need to move from ethnocentric intimacy to worldcentric intimacy with every human being, and from there to cosmocentric intimacy. This means that technology must not just take into account the discontinuity between the biosphere and the noosphere, between life and mind, but **has to be be in devotion to the *continuity* between life and mind.**

We need to honor the animal world and not eat lamb chops. Lambs are tortured for three months and not allowed to move in order to create a succulent meal for narcissistic humans, who are non-lovers because they refuse to see beyond their particular craving into the intense and unnecessary suffering of that lamb.

We need to move to cosmocentric consciousness, but we've got to do that animated by a radical positivity, with a radical thrill of the future. How can one despair when one sees that everything is unfolding and improving? When one penetrates to the inner center of becoming. True Self is *being*, but within True Self is already the seed of *becoming*. Abhinavagupta from the Kashmir Shaivism tradition talks about "the stirring of desire in the Infinite."

Let's take the Hindu version of True Self, *nirvikalpa samadhi*, where you feel a sense of complete cessation of being. That's a beautiful experience, but at some point you'll feel the stirring of desire—**the stirring of the desire of the Infinite that lives uniquely in you.** She incarnates as you, as me. Not just before Abraham *I am*, but before Abraham *I am She*.

- I am becoming.
- I am unique unfolding.
- I am unique perspective.
- I am unique intimacy.

Let's turn again to Kook, who talks about a meditative realization that's not cognitive but a non-conceptual, lived realization emergent from the interior sciences: "When one penetrates to the inner center of the becoming, ascending essence, we find there the matter of the Divine illumined with absolute brilliance, which is precisely the Infinite in action, which generates into being that which is infinite in potential." What is the Infinite in action? Here's a sentence I meditated on for the last twenty-five years, and can finally formulate clearly:

Evolution is Love-in-Action, addressing need.

When Google and Facebook hijack the best minds in the world, paying them $400,000–$500,000 a year to micro-adjust the Facebook newsfeed algorithm to make it more addictive in order to bump up their quarterly profits, **we've just drained Reality of its inherent creativity and hijacked that attention.** And remember: *it's attention that blooms Reality into being.*

The TechnoFeudal attention economy is dependent on the increasing hijacking of our attention. Not only does it make reading obsolete, shorten attention spans, and hijack the attention of the ostensible end-users of social media (who are not the end-users at all, but the fodder from whom we derive data, which then becomes the product, the basis for predictive analysis, which is then sold to people who are misaligned with those end-users). TechnoFeudalism also hijacks the attention of the best minds in the world, and focuses those minds on the narcissistic, masturbatory act of generating extra profit for a small group of people in the tech plex who don't even pay taxes.

So we need to reclaim the true nature of evolution and move from *Homo sapiens* to *Homo amor*. We need to find all the Norman Borlaugs around the world and say, "Look up, be brave, and shoot for the stars! You yourself are a star, know that you're a star. You're animated by starlight, and all of the starlight literally lives in you."

The democratization of greatness, the democratization of stardom, the democratization of enlightenment, our flickers of enlightenment: not only is the emergence of a New Human and a New Humanity a genuine option, it's the inherent movement of Cosmos itself—some place deep down we all know it's true.

The emergence of a New Human is the Infinite Intimate in action that generates into being that which is infinite in potential. Evolution shines light in all the ways of God.

But when we say God, remember that the God you don't believe in doesn't exist. It's not the traditional or medieval ethnocentric God. *This is the incessant, ceaseless creativity of Cosmos in all its personhood.* The entirety of Cosmos is evolving and ascending, just as this dynamic is recognizable in parts of it. **Every part of Cosmos is part of an interconnected, intimate whole that's actually evolving.**

- ◆ Does this mean that it all might go horribly wrong?
- ◆ Is there a horizon of existential risk that exponentiates destruction and war? All civilizations fall, so why shouldn't a global civilization fall?

- Is the Armageddon foretold by the great traditions a possibility we'll run into? The death of humanity as we know it?

All of this is a possibility if we give up, if we let our attention be hijacked, if we fail to be Outrageous Lovers. Love is a perception, a placing of attention. If we who are the avatars of the leading edge—together as a Unique Self Symphony—don't actually take our stand, of course it can all go down; we've always known that, that's nothing new. This is ours to do. **The rising of the Cosmos is universal as well as particular, collective as well as uniquely individual, eternal and evolving.**

RECLAIMING THE EMERGENCE OF GOODNESS, OUR DEEPEST HEART'S DESIRE

In the history of the Cosmos, as far as we know, until about 2,500 years ago, there's never been democracy. Until about 300 years ago, there were no universal human rights articulated to a couple of billion people who understand a growing planetary, worldcentric consciousness. This all took the entire evolutionary process millennia and centuries to manifest—and we're facing the possibility of losing it all. We're polarizing the Western world. We had NATO, and now England has left the EU. Brexit was one of the great absurdities of modernity, in which voting proved to be a sham.

In the twentieth century, a divided America coalesced around Russia as a common enemy. Our Eros was actually a pseudo-eros—**we placed Russia on the outside so we could feel like we're on the inside**. Then the Cold War collapsed, as the digital age emerged into the ascendancy in the 1980s and 1990s. Computers, with their hyper-textuality, disruption of authorship, lack of depth, and capacity to hijack attention—documented, for example, by Nicholas Carr in his book *The Shallows*—emerge alongside the postmodern mind, which fully deconstructs any notion of value.

We increasingly polarize because we have no Universal Grammar of Value.

While we're polarizing in the extreme, unable to bring Nixon and Kennedy together, all across the world, new strong men and strong women begin to emerge, and China is now in the ascendancy. China's certainly not talking about apocalypse—they are not Doomers. Instead, the Chinese Communist Party is clearly talking about the future, about world domination. This means:

+ The abandonment of liberty.
+ The abandonment of all the great values of Western democracy.
+ The abandonment of humanism.
+ The abandonment of the notion that you can speak your mind and not have someone later knock at the door.
+ The abandonment of the notion that someone like Barack Obama, whose grandfather was a day laborer, can become the leader of a powerful nation.

The dignities of the Western model have been around for only a short while, and we can lose it all. There are nations who are looking to the heavens, such as China, who are arguably participating in certain genocidal, Orwellian, totalitarian impulses and structures—none of which are rooted in the true Field of Value. While we're looking at our navels, thinking about apocalypse and doom, getting lost in *Homo sapiens* or limited versions of True Self, we abandon and betray the evolutionary impulse.

We need to reclaim the emergence of goodness.

As Abraham Kook stunningly says: "It's a given that goodness and *allness* merge into unity." Meaning: the movement of the whole thing, all of the exteriors and the interiors, is one movement, as goodness. **The All absorbs the good in each of its details. That's the inherent movement of Cosmos.**

If we awaken to this, as Cosmos, which is the only truth—anything else is ignorance—we can participate in the emergence of *Homo amor*. This is the comprehensive rising of the Cosmos; no detail will be left out, no spark will be lost from the ensemble.

Everything is being readied for this gorgeous transition. But to participate, we need a Spirit sensitized to the higher divine longing; we need to take seriously our own desire—not our surface desire, but our Deepest Heart's Desire.

Homo amor takes seriously her Deepest Heart's Desire, and knows that her Deepest Heart's Desire is the desire of She.

We are the ones we've been waiting for. It's not anybody else—*we are* the Unique Self Symphony. This is us, and this is our moment. Bono's 2020 song "We Are the People We Have Been Waiting For" has eighteen million views. The best pornography doesn't even do that well. Because this is erotica, not pornography.

This is the erotic Universe coming alive.

When people listen, they feel it and they know *we are the ones we've been waiting for.* This song exploded because everybody felt it, and knew it was true. Let's look at some of the lyrics.

SONG: "WE ARE THE PEOPLE," MARTIN GARRIX
FEATURING BONO & THE EDGE

We're a million volts in a pool of light.
Electricity in the room tonight.
Born from fire. Sparks flying from the sun.
I hardly know you. Can I confess?

I feel your heart beating in my chest.
You come with me, tonight is gonna be the one.

This is radical intimacy, where no one is a stranger—this is pure Eros.

'Cause you've faith and no fear for the fight.
You pull hope from defeat in the night.
There's an image of you in my mind.
Could be mad but you might just be right.

Homo amor just might be real.

We are the people we've been waiting for.
Out of the ruins of hate and war.
Army of lovers never seen before.
We are the people we've been waiting for.

We are the people of the open hand.
The streets of Dublin to Notre-Dame.
We'll build it better than we did before.
We are the people we've been waiting for.

Yes, there are pieces that are broken in religion.

Broken bells at a broken church.
Heart that hurts is a heart that works.

There's nothing more whole than a broken heart. **It's only when the heart breaks that the heart breaks *open*.**

From a broken place. That's where victory is won.

You can't get to the post-tragic unless you walk directly through the tragic—avoidance never works.

'Cause you've faith and no fear for the fight.
You pull hope from defeat in the night.
There's an image of you in my mind.
Could be mad but you might just be right.

We are the people we've been waiting for.
Out of the ruins of hate and war.
Army of lovers never seen before.
We are the people we've been waiting for.

2.7

THE THREE SELVES: *HOMO AMOR* IS A MEMORY OF THE FUTURE

In terms of an expanded and evolving sense of identity, there are three fundamental selves—and *Homo amor* has to embrace all of them. In some sense, they're all part of this larger one, without which we can't walk into the future.

THE PSYCHOLOGICAL SELF

The first is what we call psychological self, the self that embraces the past, a reflection of the brilliant innovations of twentieth-century psychology. Modernity brought us many tragedies, but also many dignities, and part of it was this great realization that the past itself can grab the steering wheel of my life—and **if I go back to the past and re-animate that moment, I can actually heal trauma**. This is a beautiful and important realization.

Freud's teacher Breuer understood that the "hysterical" women he treated were not deranged or evil, but were actually traumatized, and often sexually abused. So he went back and worked with the past. The psychological self sees the past as a place which has great treasure. That's the brilliant insight of psychology: a re-embracing and re-framing of the past. That's psychological self.

THE MYSTICAL SELF

We might call the second self the classical enlightenment self, or True Self, but let's just call it mystical self for now. It says, "Don't look at the past, that's just a story. Don't get lost in that story. Abandon your therapist or your psychologist, come to the ashram. You've been doing therapy, and that didn't really get you very far, did it? Step into the power of the now and it will dissolve your pain body."

Of course, the mystical self is saying something very real that the psychological self doesn't understand. In fact, each of these—the mystical and the psychological self—are reverently in devotion to a First Principle of Cosmos.

The First Principle and First Value of Cosmos that the psychological self honors is the past. **The past is not just a moment in time, but a First Principle and First Value of Cosmos.**

That's why the emergence of history is the evolution of consciousness; the emergence of history is the realization that the past reverentially matters. Now of course, every First Principle and First Value has a shadow aspect to it. We can get obsessively lost in the past. Collectively, this means we can go the route of fascism and reconstruct a contrived history in order to be loyal to a past, but be brutal in the present. On an individual level, we can also get lost in the loops of the past and keep reliving old patterns and be stuck in those old ways of being, unable to access and capacitate new ways. Of course there are shadows. But the First Principle of the past is psychological self.

The mystical self is the First Principle and First Value of the present. The present is filled with wonder, with the ceaseless eternity of the present. Ceaseless eternity is not everlasting time. As Wittgenstein said, "Eternity is beneath time." It's what we meant when we said that the unjust death of one human being and the death of humanity are both equal challenges; one is not more or less than the other—because both demand that we get beneath and beyond time.

That's the True Self, the mystical self *of the timeless time and the placeless place, resting in the divine embrace.* That's the First Principle and First Value of the present.

EVOLUTIONARY UNIQUE SELF

Ultimately, we need to go further and embrace *Homo amor. Homo amor* not only holds a memory of the past and heals Reality by healing the past, and *Homo amor* not only merely steps into the present as mystical self, but *Homo amor* **transcends and includes both psychological self and mystical self, emerging as Evolutionary Unique Self.**

In this way *Homo amor* reclaims hope—because hope is a memory of the future. *Homo amor* is a memory of the future. CosmoErotic Humanism is a memory of the future.

The entire future—trillions upon trillions of people—have but one voice to speak for them, and that's us. We're holding the memory of their future. To look down instead of looking up—in a narcissistic, self-absorbed way is to ignore this truth of the future whose voice we are. Instead we need to look up and into the faces of the trillions of future souls who are calling our name. We need not only to explore options in outer space, we need to go into inner space in order to generate a New Human and a New Humanity. Not to do so is a betrayal of the future. The past is real, and the present is real, but to avoid the future is to betray the future.

When we incarnate a memory of the future, we find love in a hopeless place. We've moved from the tragic to the post-tragic, and we can truly feel what Yeats was saying:

> *When such as we cast out remorse,*
> *So great a sweetness fills our breast.*
> *We can dance, and we can sing.*
> *We are blest by everything.*
> *Everything we look upon is blest.*

CHAPTER 3

ARE WE WELCOME IN COSMOS? THE MOTHER AND THE BIRTH OF HOMO AMOR IN EARLY BIBLICAL CONSCIOUSNESS

3.1

RECLAIMING PRAYER FROM THE DEPTHS OF SILENCE

Prayer has gotten a bad reputation in the last little while—but mostly because it has been done poorly. The way we typically pray is to the "cosmic vending-machine god," whom we often think is owned only by our religion: we put in a quarter, and hope to get something good in return. That's a bribe, that's corrupt—it doesn't work.

The god you don't believe in doesn't exist.

True prayer is when we find the deepest place in our heart and understand that Divinity is not just the Infinity of Power but the Infinity of Intimacy.

Feel into the most intimate moment that you ever had, alone or with others. Now exponentialize that intimacy and realize that all intimacy participates in the larger field of intimacy. Now turn to the Infinite Intimate, to that expansive field, and say, "Oh my God, could you hold my *holy and broken Hallelujah*? Could you hold the whole thing for me? Could you hold it with me?"

Before prayer, let's rest for a second, not in the silence of absence, but in Silence of Presence.

What's the difference? Say you're on a date that has gone very badly, you're driving back at the end, and it's just not working. If there was an eject button, you'd get the person out of the car. This terrible silence descends because there's really nothing left to say. That's a silence of absence, where you are desperate for any word to cover over the emptiness always lurking in your life.

You keep yourself so busy, so engaged, so medicated, and so creative as it were, to avoid at all costs that emptiness. But now the silence of absence bursts through.

But there is the second kind of silence that we recognize just as well, *a silence that is filled with love.* Say there was some love back in high school or college with someone and you hadn't seen them in a long time. It's now twenty years later and you meet them randomly on the corner. You start talking, and then keep talking and talking. Then you sit down, have a cup of coffee, and suddenly it's nine hours later... You've been on the inside of the inside, this timeless time, this placeless place. Now you're in the car again, she's driving you to the train, and a rich and loving and pure silence descends on the car.

It's the most beautiful silence in the entire world. This is the Silence of Presence we're going to enter now.

From that place we engage in prayer, desperately, with full heart, full Eros.

Our prayer is a song, a sacred text of culture that invites us deeper and deeper into intimacy.

PRAYER: "I WANT TO KNOW WHAT LOVE IS," FOREIGNER

We're on the inside, with full heart, like we've never prayed before. From the Silence of Presence, in the space between the breaths. From this place, let's read this sacred text of culture "I Want To Know What Love Is." Although Foreigner probably didn't intend to write a "prayer," they did anyway. So with these words, we pray...

In my life, there's been heartache and pain
I don't know if I can face it again
Can't stop now, I've traveled so far
To change this lonely life

I wanna know what love is
I want you to show me
I wanna feel what love is
I know you can show me

I wanna know what love is...

3.2

RECAPITULATION: A VISION OF A NEW HUMAN AND A NEW HUMANITY

We're now deeply aware of the Reality of existential risk. We understand the risks posed by diffusely distributed exponential technology among state and non-state actors, and we know that if any one of them is fulfilled, then humanity as we know it, perhaps within fifty to 100 years—or sooner—will cease to exist. We're not facing *the first shock of existence*, which is the realization we're individually going to die. It's not just a realization of biological death which pressed us into inner space and generated all of human civilization, but rather *the second shock of existence, the death of humanity as a genuine option*.

But we're not plunged into despair or hopelessness. We don't look down, we look up. *We're inspired, exhilarated, called forth, pressed into service.*

We both reach for outer space, as Branson and Bezos recently did in their rockets, and we also reach for *inner* space, as took place during the Renaissance in sixteenth-century Florence—that great time between worlds and between stories, during which there was this realization that

the only way to move forward amid the collapse of structures and great threats to the known world was to *tell a New Story*.

This is not a made-up story, but the best integration of all dimensions of wisdom—traditional, modern, and postmodern. The Renaissance was the best integration of all traditions of wisdom that lived until the time of da Vinci and Ficino, combined with all of the best knowledge of art and science. This allowed for a radically different way of seeing the world differently and telling a new story: modernity.

This story enabled new exterior technologies that resulted in a new way of understanding the intimate, participatory relationship between the human mind and the world: Kepler and Galileo's laws of motion, much of the modern medicine and science we all live with and take for granted today, and all of the greatness and dignities of modernity. Yet, the fault lines in the story, the missing actors and dimensions, inevitably assured that it would hit a wall.

As the exterior technologies were emerging, a set of interior technologies developed in concert:

- Feminism and equal rights among men and women.
- Universal human rights, which had never existed before.
- A movement from ethnocentric intimacy—the love of my tribe and my people—to worldcentric intimacy, the sense that every human being is at play and in play.

Incredible, gorgeous, stunning breakthroughs in interior technologies took place for a couple hundred years. And then they stopped. But the exterior technologies kept rushing forward. We went from the Industrial Revolution to the world of infotech, exploding from half a billion people to nearly eight billion, all based on **a new core story of success: rivalrous conflict governed by win-lose metrics**, the necessity of the individual to achieve, stand out, out-compete, and succeed. This story replaced the success story prominent in premodernity, which basically said that you had to obey (your local, tribal) God.

116

EXPONENTIAL TECHNOLOGY, RIVALROUS
CONFLICT, AND PLANETARY BOUNDARIES

This new story of success worked pretty well in a non-globalized world of non-exponential technology. However, it has taken us directly to where we are today, a world of exponential technology and rivalrous conflict driving our extraction-based model to run up against planetary boundaries, all in a period of about thirty to sixty years—exhausting what took the planet billions of years to manifest. This has set the stage for the sixth mass extinction of life on earth. That's a big deal.

Given this context, we can look away, *or we can turn towards and actually step in.*

We can face the second shock of existence, and let it blow our hearts open like they've never been opened before. Just like da Vinci and his cohort, we can introduce a new vision of art and science. But most importantly, we can introduce *an emergent new vision of what it means to be a human being on planet earth*—and the good news is that it's the nature of Reality for us to do so, for human beings will not remain as we are. The Cosmos' trajectory from matter to life to mind—matter triumphs in life, life triumphs in mind—suggests that mind itself must also triumph.

The human being as *Homo sapiens* doesn't go on forever; either we hit the planetary boundaries, or we transcend.

A vision emerges of a New Human and a New Humanity: Homo sapiens becomes Homo amor.

Who is *Homo amor*? To answer that question, we first must situate ourselves: We are at the leading edge of consciousness. We are aware of being in a time between worlds and a time between stories, as most of the world goes on doing business as usual, precisely as it happened in Florence. Though they sometimes laughed at da Vinci, he understood that the world as they knew it would not continue. He could see around the corner, and while most people thought premodernity would go on forever, he understood that wasn't true. He built new statues, he made new art, and he created new science that attempted to raise all boats, and largely succeeded.

We're again at that moment where evolution generates new emergence. This is not miraculous in the sense that it violates the natural order of the world. This *is* the natural order of the world. Reality generates new emergence, and emergency always generates emergence. *Our crisis is a birth, and an evolutionary driver.*

The narcissist may ignore the crisis, but that doesn't mean the crisis isn't here. That's not our move. Instead:

- We're at the leading edge.
- We're madly in love with each other.
- We're madly in love with Reality.
- We're not willing to limit our love to the one or two or three people that we met. That's egocentric love.
- We're going to love widely.
- We're going to be Outrageous Evolutionary Lovers.

We're going to love Reality itself, understanding that the quality of Love is not small, ordinary love. It's what Dante called "the love that moves the sun and other stars." It's what Tagore was describing when he said: "Love is not mere human sentiment—it's the heart of existence itself." In other words, love is not a strategy to cover over the emptiness. Love is a disclosure of the true nature of Reality—what we have called the CosmoErotic Universe.

It's the love that's the heart of existence itself, the love that flames alive in me as I feel the full *Fuck* of the Cosmos moving through me, throbbing, pulsing, waking me up.

It's *that* love we need to bring as we step in.

3.3

THE STRUCTURE OF THE INTIMATE UNIVERSE: IS THERE A WELCOME HOME SIGN IN THE UNIVERSE?

Albert Einstein was a wild and crazy man. A brilliant scientist, he said a lot of great things about physics. But he said many not so brilliant things about other topics, and yet because he was a physicist he was given a lot of credit. Just as there's dogmatism in religion, there's dogmatism in science. Because physics is the Rolls-Royce of science, from a mechanistic physicalist paradigm, if we look—as physics does—at the smallest, most elemental structures of Reality, we may think we're looking at *all* of Reality. Because physicists study science, they've become the new priests. **Just as we assigned priests authority they shouldn't have had, we assign physicists authority that they shouldn't have, because of our closet materialism.**

That being said, Einstein did intuit something unbelievably important outside the realm of physics. At the end of a long interview, a reporter once asked him, "If you could ask one question, if you wanted to know one thing, what would be the most important question you would ask?" Einstein answered, "I think I would ask: **is the Universe friendly or not?**"

Put slightly differently: **Are we welcome in the Universe?** Is the universe friendly to us, or is it indifferent? Are we a chance happenstance passing through? Is the Universe "a tale told by an idiot full of sound and fury signifying nothing?"

Is there a welcome sign in the Universe? It's a great question. If there is a welcome sign, it means: Welcome home, this is where we're *supposed* to be. **There's meaning everywhere. The Universe is alive. Reality is a symphony of significance, wonder, and beauty.**

In my experience, we are absolutely welcome in the universe. What a mother most wants to give her children, what I want to give my children as a father, is a sense that they're welcome in the Universe, that there's a "welcome home" sign in Cosmos. Sometimes you go to someone's house, and they greet you at the door, "Welcome, welcome," but you don't feel all that welcome. Or sometimes we do—we can know the difference in our bodies.

Later in life, if we're lucky, we start to realize that details from past experience are embedded in our bodies. We remember the traumas—*the body keeps the score*, as Bessel van der Kolk put it. We remember everything and we need to do that work. **That work is not going to change existential risk, and it won't blow me out in joy—but it's very important work.**

For example, my parents fought a lot. They'd be in the middle of a huge argument and the doorbell would ring. All of a sudden, they would have big smiles on their faces and say, "Welcome, welcome." I remember hearing that welcome and thinking, "Wow, no one's really welcome here."

Have you ever done someone a favor, and they say, "Thank you," and then you say, "You're welcome." Why? They just said, "Thank you." Are you welcoming them to your house for a party? What does that mean? It's almost as bad as when someone asks, "How are you?" and the polite non-response is, "Fine, and how are you?" A lot of the time no one wants to know how you are. Someone says, "How are you?" and you say, "I so appreciate you asking that question. Let me tell you how I am." Their stomachs fall. They're not really asking how you are. So why are we saying, "you're welcome?" We will get to that question.

Even with all the veneer of civilization, do we *really* feel welcome? If not, how might we feel this cosmic welcome?

THE PSEUDO-EROS OF POLARIZATION IN A GLOBAL CONTEXT

Why is the world so disastrously politically divided? Because of **polarization**. Many think: "I'm absolutely certain I'm right, and you're wrong." That's polarization, of which we have more today than ever, and which is blocking us from getting anything done. We're at a moment where **every existential risk requires global coordination and global coherence**. You can't deal with Covid within the framework of your country's boundaries because the virus happens to not respect national boundaries.

It is utterly absurd to think that a nation-state alone can deal with a virus that came from gain-of-function research in Wuhan, organized by the United States and China, which propagated all over the world without bothering with national/nation state boundaries.

The reason there is massive starvation and great suffering in certain parts of Africa today, is because each nation-state deals with issues by itself. Mothers are watching their children die, while everyone else deals with their petty Covid challenges, wrapped up in their own narcissism because we didn't figure out how to have a coherent, coordinated response to a clearly global issue.

There is no serious existential risk, pandemic or otherwise, today, which is not global.

121

Without global coherence and global coordination, it is impossible to respond to any of the massive risks that challenge us. **What blocks global coordination is polarization, which is the opposite of intimacy.** We say the root problem is a "global intimacy disorder," founded in something very deep: We're all stuck in our certainties.

Let's explore the quality of *Homo amor*. How does the New Human and the New Humanity relate to certainty and uncertainty? What is the next level of human consciousness?

Just as the view of certainty and uncertainty in the traditional period saw faith and certainty as gorgeous and uncertainty as the devil, in the modern period the only certainty that was said to exist is the proof that results from scientific experiment, whereas everything else embraces uncertainty. But as modernity has continued to unfold, it wasn't enough just to have certainty about scientific issues; we began to polarize ever more intensely, and we felt the need to create national identities.

A hundred years ago, during World War I, France and Germany stood across from one other, separated by five hundred feet, and sent four million people to their deaths, spurred on by extreme polarization within the community of nation-states.

The strategy of being on the inside by placing somebody else outside is what we do when we don't have real Eros. We create pseudo-eros by drawing a circle and saying, "I'm inside the circle, you're outside." During the Cold War, as long as Russia was outside the circle, we were inside and our identity was formed by our enemy. Over the last thirty years, though, as the Cold War has died away, NATO fighting Russia wasn't the game anymore—although this has come back in a new way—which meant we could no longer pseudo-erotically form our identity through in-group/out-group dynamics. That's not Eros, that's pseudo-Eros:

- You're not in Eros.
- You're not in the flow and current of Cosmos.
- You're not in the Field of Value.

- You're not on the inside of the inside.
- You want the illusion of being on the inside—by placing somebody else on the outside.

When Russia collapsed, all of a sudden the West had no enemy, and we could no longer identify ourselves based on the Other, based on who is outside the circle. We subsequently began to retribalize and polarize—in the U.S., for example, we repolarized into red states and blue states. Once again we created an Other in order to place them outside the circle and give ourselves the illusion that we are inside. **We were *seduced* into rivalrous dynamics as a form of identity formation.** This rivalrous conflict has been governed by dangerous win/lose metrics. As a result, there is no global coherence, no coordination—the shared Field of Value is fractured.

> *We have forgotten that everyone is welcome in the Universe, as part of the shared Field of Value.*

As a direct result of the collapse of a shared global grammar of value, the global economy is destabilizing, moving towards systems collapse, and the same is true with democratic structures of governance. There's a grievous loss of coherence, and an abdication of responsibility.

As an example, many people knew Covid was about to happen two months before it hit the news. All the leaders should have gotten together and stated, "We know a serious global illness is coming, we have about six weeks, and we're coordinating our resources and our medical efforts. Rest assured, we're all part of the human race, we've got this handled together." Why was there no conference? Why was there no coordination? Radical national polarization cost us more than five million lives, economic devastation for generations, and a tremendous amount of unnecessary suffering. **We couldn't coordinate—there was no shared story, no shared Field of**

Value, just radical polarization. Instead, we were caught up in global action paralysis and confusion.

When there's radical polarization, when there's no shared Field of Value, you can't feel you are truly welcome. When you're not welcome in the Eros that animates Reality, you create pseudo-eros.

Polarization comes from pseudo-eros, which always plays out when there's no Eros. When you believe you're in the empty space of no Eros—and we can't live without Eros—then false identification causes you to act out in every possible form. Acting out is not necessarily bad, but it's just pseudo-eros most of the time. If it's true, clarified Eros, go for it all the way.

If we're stuck in the pseudo-erotic—covering over the emptiness by repeating the same things that aren't filling me up, that aren't blowing my heart open, that aren't loving me open into my beauty and loving Reality open into its beauty, then *nothing's* getting loved open. When we're just repeating the same thing again and again, then we need to shift to true and clarified Eros. **Pseudo-eros, the polarization into us/them identities, happens when we're outside the Field of Value, outside the Field of Eros.**

How do we enter the field of Eros? As in the Renaissance, this new human being emerges at this moment of existential risk. We can't rely only on the enlightened few anymore—*we need the democratization of enlightenment, of greatness.*

We must access Eros as the core quality of Reality.

That's our overarching issue.

We're going to enter through the door of *welcome*. **What does it mean to actually be welcome? What does it mean to move beyond the traumas**

we all have of not being or feeling welcome? How do we *fall into Reality* and have the experience of being welcome?

THE EXISTENTIALISTS: "WE ARE NOT WELCOME..."

Recall that the existentialists—Sartre, Camus, and all the rest—completely believed that **we're not welcome in Cosmos, alone in a vast and empty Universe.** But, they said, even though we're not welcome, let's try and be heroic about it. The existential literature beautifully rebelled against the old religion. In much of Europe, the existential literature still dominates culture, even though most people have never read an existentialist text. The existential literature was in many ways appropriately rebelling against the old religion, but what is it saying?

In the old religion there was a deep sense of welcome, but you were welcome *only* if you were from my religion, you did the same rituals, and you went to my church. Nobody else was welcome.

So the existentialists correctly challenged that, but they went a bit too far and claimed that actually therefore no one is welcome in Cosmos: "The Universe is empty, but let's try and get along without being welcome." That didn't go so well for Sartre and Camus and all the rest—it results in the sense of what Sartre calls "nausea," an inability, we might say, to access the core structure of Reality, the Field of Value, in which I actually know that I'm welcome.

FEELING WELCOME THROUGH THE UNIQUE WONDER OF THE BODY

When you relax for a second—out of the dogmas of scientific materialism and existential literature, and into your life in this moment—you can access, directly through both the exterior and interior sciences, through an apprehension of the world and through your own field of feeling, *the experience of being welcome in Reality.*

It's right there, always.

Here you are. Feel into this:

- Your body has about thirty-seven trillion cells.
- Each one of those cells is distinct and unique—both the same as everyone else's, and completely distinct, unlike any other cell in the world.
- Each one of those cells is a cacophony of complexity, beauty, and dazzling brilliance.
- Each one operates, individually and in concert, with much more intelligence and wisdom than the most sophisticated AI machine-learning algorithm in the world today.
- You've got trillions upon trillions upon trillions of neurons that are allured to, erotically entangled with, and engaged in conversation with each other.
- Let's not even talk about the astounding number of atoms, all in erotic dance with each other, all in glorious harmony.
- That entire structure is sustaining you, holding you, nurturing you, breathing you, living you in this very second now.
- In this very second, right now, the most sophisticated, erotic, stunning, living, pulsing Eros is moving and animating your unique being in a way that it doesn't animate anyone else.
- You are irreducibly unique and yet completely connected, part of the whole thing.

You're fully autonomous, utterly unique, and yet indivisible from the entire system. No one exists independently of anything else. The individual is thus an "optical delusion of consciousness" (that's the second major thing Einstein got right).

You're completely inter-penetrated with the whole thing, but even before this interpenetration, you are always already animated, held, loved, nurtured, adored, caressed, stroked, fed by every single cell, neuron, atom, molecular structure in your **individuated body** that's now fully in play in this very second.

WE ARE PART OF THE SAME FIELD

We participate together in some sense in the same field. When you say "Thank you," what you're saying is… "It's not just win/lose metrics. It's not rivalrous conflict. You did something for me? Thank you." But often we think, okay, I did something for you, and it's win/lose metrics, so now you owe me. Isn't that how many of us think? I did someone a business favor, I took them out to dinner—who doesn't have some gauge in their mind that does an immediate calculation? I just did something for someone, and by the logic of win-lose metrics, they now owe me.

But that's not the way we want to play.

When we say "Thank you" and receive "You're welcome"—we know it's not reducible to win/lose metrics. You're welcome, we're welcome, together.

- ◆ We're part of the same field.
- ◆ We participate and live together as the same seamless coat of the Universe.
- ◆ We're not separate from each other—our brains are entrained, our muons and atoms and neurons are dancing together.
- ◆ We couldn't live without each other—we in-breathe and out-breathe each other, together.
- ◆ Nothing is separate from anything else—that's the root of systems theory.

That's how we understand an entangled, intimate universe, from the quantum level up. That's radical intimacy.

127

As Zen Master Dogen said, "Enlightenment means intimacy with all things." Said differently, in economic terms, enlightenment means there are no externalities. Nothing and no one is on the outside. "You did something for me? Thank you." How do you respond? "You're welcome," which means: **there are no strangers anywhere in the Cosmos.** The physicists were correct in describing in terms of physics what Meister Eckhart knew in terms of the interior sciences: *The universe is making love in every second.*

All of Reality—all the way up, and all the way down—is lines and circles, interpenetrating everywhere all at once.

Intimacy means shared identity: I literally can't survive without you, my identity, my existence depends on you. And not just you. Without the mollusks at the bottom of the ocean, without insects in the ground, without the fungus in the forest, I literally don't exist. Without the entire biosphere there's no me. I have no identity without the coral reefs. And I certainly have no identity without you.

Love discloses the nature of Reality. The fundamental nature of Reality is shared identity.

But it's not only shared identity. Let's recall the intimacy equation:

> *Intimacy = shared identity in the context of (relative) otherness x mutuality of recognition (we recognize each other) x mutuality of pathos (we feel each other) x mutuality of value (we live in a shared Field of Value) x mutuality of purpose (we share goals and meaning).*

I don't exist without you, and to believe that I do is suicide. The universe every second is quite literally breathing me open. In terms of chemical structure, atmospheric structure, biological structure, molecular structure, we're being breathed into life in every second. **Reality is screaming "welcome" to me, to us, literally, every nanosecond.**

A SHARED FIELD OF VALUE IS NEEDED TO ADDRESS INTERCONNECTED PROBLEMS

Drop in, open the Eye of the Heart, and feel that sense of shared identity. When I say "thank you," it's not an act of manipulation that I gave you a gift; we're exchanging gifts every second *because that's actually the nature of Reality itself.*

This is why no problem can truly be solved without solving all other (interconnected) problems. It is one large system of intimate relationships, so if we solve only one problem while ignoring the larger whole, we create externalities. **Only when we recognize all problems as part of the same shared identity can we begin to work towards resolution.** If the problems are not experienced as intimate with one another—as part of the same field—then new problems are generated by solving the first problem, and often the new problem is more ominous than the first one we were trying to solve.

For example, if we're addressing climate change, we may propose planting more trees to sequester more carbon in the atmosphere. This is a good idea, and yet if we do, current agricultural practices demand large amounts of fertilizer, and the nitrates from the fertilizer pour into the ocean and create more dead zones—a new solution may ignore or exacerbate existing, interconnected problems, or create new ones—because we have no felt sense of intimacy between the problems. Each problem is mistakenly seen as discrete, alienated from the larger field of intimacy in which all problems share an identity, are inter-included with each other.

To the extent that Borlaug was not successful in solving world hunger, it was because we lacked an understanding of this overall context. He and the Green Revolution are often seen as the ultimate example of the progress narrative. But a more careful look shows that Borlaug and his pesticides created a host of problems, the depth of which may far exceed the challenges he solved.

We don't yet intuitively realize that *every part is connected to every other part,* that the notion of the "part" is an artificial construction, an illusion.

Or let's say we wish to create a carbon tax—that's a great idea, we should do it, and it'll certainly help reduce carbon emissions. But because of interconnection, we must anticipate second- and third-order consequences beyond the immediate effects. Initially, perhaps, only the Western nations will sign it; China may not sign it, as a result of which their GDP may go up, and they'll use the revenue to further their own geopolitical and military goals—which will have their own consequences. Without the perspective of shared identity, deep entangled intimacy, and a shared Field of Value, decontextualized ideas and plans like this are simply insufficient.

What we're now realizing is that the structure of the intimate universe, in which nothing exists independently of anything else, is also the structure of our geopolitical and economic reality. Until the end of the second World War, the entire physical structure of the world was of course completely interconnected—but nations were geographically separated. That's no longer true. The 1944 Bretton Woods conference reorganized the world: we've created supply lines, economic interdependencies, and currency interdependencies that never before existed in Reality. The Old World is gone, and a physical public Reality exists that mirrors our collective interior Reality. Now, with the scale of our interconnected global systems, you can no longer solve any problem independent of any other problem, which is why:

- You can't solve any problem unless you have **coherence.**
- You can't have coherence unless you have **intimacy.**
- You can't have intimacy unless you have **a shared Field of Value.**

This is the heart of the matter. And we can only begin to see this by stepping back and realizing: *we're all welcome in the Cosmos together.*

Underneath the surface polarization, Reality is saying welcome to each and every one of us, and to all of us together, at every level. It's beautiful. **There**

are no strangers in Reality—everyone's already a friend. That's the structure of Reality we know in the exterior sciences—in physics, in chemistry, in molecular biology. But it's also the interior structure of Reality.

There are no strangers in the universe.

The old religions were mostly wrong about this. The "welcome home" sign in the Cosmos is not only for the Jews, or the Christians, or for Muslims. The movement from ethnocentric to worldcentric intimacy is based on the realization that *everybody's welcome.*

MOTHER IS ANOTHER WORD FOR WELCOME

We can say that another word for welcome is "Mother." When I'm born into the world, I meet my biological mother, what does the mother say to me? *The mother says "welcome home."* If our mother doesn't say this, our whole life changes. This is where our first feelings of welcome arise—or fail to arise.

Perhaps one of the most important psychological theories from the last couple of decades, attachment theory, centers around one issue: **Did I experience my mother saying "Welcome home" to me?** If not, then until I somehow remember or rediscover this, the rest of my life is going to derail: my attachment style will either be marked by insecurity, anxiety, or avoidance. We've lost touch with this knowledge over the last few hundred years. So it's not by accident that attachment theory has emerged to tell us that our psychological state is based on the nature of the "Welcome home" sign your mother put over your crib.

Whether you're able to be lived as love, in its best sense, comes from your early experience of the universe, initially mediated by your mother. But to the innovators in attachment theory and many others, there's an increasing realization that the sense of Mother is much bigger than the biological mother. **The Mother is much closer to the felt sense of being welcome in** the Cosmos. For all its great insights, attachment theory places inordinately too much emphasis on the biological mother and then collapses mental health around this one relationship.

As significant as this early connection is, the true welcome home sign comes not from your mother or what your mother did.

The biological mother is but one of a hundred billion expressions of the Mother.

The practice of life is knowing, finding, and accessing this truth *everywhere*, **realizing that I'm welcome even here, right now, that** *I'm always already home.* If we don't feel there's a fundamental welcome home sign in the Cosmos, then we can't be welcome *anywhere*. If we're not primordially welcome, then any other attempt to feel welcome in our own little world is going to collapse and fail eventually.

• • •

If we don't begin to realize there's a fundamental welcome home sign in the Cosmos, all contrived "Welcome home" signs disappear. We lose the sense of connection, and everyone becomes a stranger. Indeed, Camus's book *The Stranger* opens with the sentence: "Mother died today, or was it yesterday. I can't be sure." On the first page of one of his most important books, he's saying that if there's no welcome home sign in Cosmos, as the existentialists believed, **then the Mother doesn't really matter**. What's supposed to be the most revered thing in the world, the first experience of a child, just doesn't matter. "My mother died today or was it yesterday? I don't know, what's the difference?"

We need a welcome home sign in the Cosmos in order to know that we are enough. **And we are absolutely enough, regardless of whether or not any of our individual mothers did a good job.**

We can find another example in the world of psychedelic therapy. Michael Pollan wrote a great book called *How to Change Your Mind*, about the power of plant medicine. We learn that ayahuasca is commonly referred to as "the Mother" because the plant commonly does one thing: It often, ultimately gives a person the experience of being held in deep, radical love, and all conflict falls away. **We get the direct experience of being held in the arms of the Mother. No matter where we are, we fall into her hands**.

Similarly, when I go to the ocean, I feel that it holds me. That's why the ocean is seen as a maternal force in all the mystical traditions. Why do we gaze at the ocean? We gaze at the ocean because *the ocean welcomes us home*.

GOODNESS, TRUTH, AND BEAUTY ARE WELCOME HOME SIGNS

Nature welcomes me, the ocean welcomes me, and beauty welcomes me. Beauty is a powerful welcome home sign—and not just because of the gorgeousness of symmetry. In theories of beauty, symmetry is just one form of beauty. But a color is also beauty—a gorgeous color welcomes me home: a deep purple, a gorgeous orange, a rich scarlet. Have you ever looked at the colors of moths and butterflies? They're stunning, simply marvelous. Beauty and color are signs from the Cosmos telling me I'm welcome here.

Truth is another welcome home sign, as witnessed in mathematics, so elegant because our minds are mathematically aligned with this higher truth. Human science works because, as Cosmic humans, we are fundamentally welcome in the universe. Ramanujan was a great young mathematician from India who died in his early thirties, and whom Hardy received in Cambridge. He later said about Ramanujan that he was intimate with every integer in the universe, that *every number in the world welcomed him*. This is the welcome of mathematics, as it describes the fundamental Eros of the Cosmos.

The experience of goodness is when I do something for someone not because I'm guided by win-lose metrics—thank you, you're welcome—but because we feel each other! **The utter delight I get when I do something that's good, that fills my body, that opens me up, tells me I am aligned with Cosmos.**

Goodness, Truth, and Beauty are welcome home signs. As they evolve, the welcome home sign evolves.

Artists, scientists, men and women of Spirit, despite all the divisions between the sciences, the arts, and spiritual practice—are all engaged in the same thing. They're all putting up welcome home signs all over Cosmos. If you want to trace Reality, you can feel the welcome home signs everywhere. **The welcome home sign is not for any specific group, but for all of us.** We all participate in that welcome; we all have intrinsic value. The ocean is the Mother and She welcomes us. Goodness, Truth, and Beauty always lead us back to the knowledge that we are welcome home in the Cosmos.

RECONSTRUCTING THE FIELD OF VALUE

Modernity, existentialism, and postmodernity have each deconstructed a piece of value, every step along the way. In some respects, this is a valuable and necessary function, a welcome challenge to outdated dogma. However, if we don't then engage in a *reconstructive* project in which Goodness, Truth, and Beauty are seen once again as the intrinsic values of Cosmos— if we view beauty as merely contrived; if we view truth as purely made up; if we view goodness as a social construction (the position expressed by writers like Yuval Harari)—then we are lost:

- We'll witness the further entrenchment of tribalization and polarization, and lose the possibility of global coordination or coherence.
- Rivalrous win/lose metrics will continue to rule our culture, and pseudo-eros will continue to pervade.

◆ If we can't step fully into Eros, the only things left are **pseudo-erotic fictions** and social constructions of Reality.

This is the story we're in right now. We've lost the ability to articulate a Universal Grammar of Value, a shared story of Goodness, Truth, and Beauty, through which we reconstruct our understanding of Reality. **We've forgotten that Goodness, Truth, and Beauty are not just eternal, but they're also** *evolving* **values intrinsic to Cosmos**—and that we're all always held together by the Mother.

At the moment, everyone is seen as a stranger in Cosmos. Camus' diagnosis in *The Stranger* was correct—*Mother died today, or was it yesterday*—because we've slain the Mother, and all contemporary pseudo-erotic attempts to resurrect her, born of win/lose metrics, are doomed from the start. We have to reclaim the Mother because if there's no welcome in Cosmos, there's no welcome anywhere in life.

Then we're all just exchanging favors: "Thank you—(*now you owe me*)." **We need to shift to: "thank you—you're welcome—(*we're part of the same universal Field of Value*)."**

You cannot understand either molecular biology or biochemistry, or molecular physics, or systems theory as it operates in physics and economics, without this sense of welcome, without understanding that this Universe is intimately interwoven, without understanding that we do not exist independently of anything else, without understanding that **we're being welcomed and breathed open molecularly, atomically, cellularly, intersubjectively—every second. These are the bases of life that animate all of us.**

We don't need the mystics to tell us this—this is just the science of the day. There is so much magnificence in the ocean, as that evocative song tells us. Every human being has a right to know that they're welcome in Cosmos, that they're embraced in the arms of the Mother every second.

3.4

ENLIGHTENMENT IS INTIMACY WITH ALL THINGS

One thing we could say is: The global intimacy disorder is a failure of intimacy between physics and the humanities. Of course, physics has to operate according to its laws, its structures of validation, and its principles. The human sciences also have to operate according to their laws. But Goodness, Truth, and Beauty—signs of the moral universe, the ethos of the universe—are "welcome home signs" in the Cosmos.

A global intimacy disorder has emerged because we've forgotten our cosmic welcome. The scientists now need to become the new poets, mystics, and musicians. Ramanujan said he could hear the musical note of every number in the Universe. It was Pythagoras who understood that music is the mathematics of intimacy. We can add that mathematics is the music of Reality.

The global intimacy disorder is between us and the split-off parts of ourselves which go into shadow and scream at us that we're not welcome. This disorder is based on win-lose metrics, as we're constantly exchanging favors and goods hoping to somehow stand out, triumph, be recognized, and feel welcome. However...

We're always already welcome. The universe is actually madly in love with us, loving us personally and insanely in every moment—and that's not merely a spiritual idea or a declaration of faith. It's the essential nature of Cosmos itself.

Einstein was correct. The experience of the separate self is but an optical delusion of consciousness. In that sense, we speak of the Democratization of Enlightenment—it is not a pristine accomplishment undertaken by the elite few. No, it is one simple thing—*Enlightenment is sanity*. **To be sane is to have a taste of Enlightenment, to let my life be enlivened by the ocean, to feel every cell in my body alive and pulsing, to be connected with the wider field.**

To be sane means to know Reality. If I tell you that I'm Prince William of England, you'd likely say, "He's insane. He thinks he's Prince William, and he's definitely not, that's for sure." It's a failure of identity. I actually don't know who I am.

Sanity is to know my identity. It's to know who I am—and who I am is not a separate self, but a part of the whole, interconnected with everything. Our apparent separation is a delusion. I'm infused and inextricably bound up with the top-soil and the insects in it, without which I'm literally not alive. I'm inextricably bound up with forms of plant life that I've never heard of, without which I can't survive.

I'm inextricably bound up with the entire biosphere, which lives in me even as I live in the biosphere. I'm basically committing suicide when experiencing myself as lost in the parameters of my own narcissism of my separate-self life and its win-lose metrics. I don't feel the Universe enfolding me and welcoming me, so I tribalize, polarize, and place other people outside the circle—and then I can be inside the circle, competing all the time in order just to feel that I exist.

No. Enlightenment is sanity, true intimacy with all things. In economic terms, enlightenment means there are no "externalities." When a company attends only to its financial bottom line and ignores its impact on the environment, its impact on the lives of its employees, its impact on its competitors, its impact on the commons... to ignore that is worse than narcissism—it's insanity. So in this case sanity means realizing that nothing is external.

Enlightenment means intimacy with all things, and intimacy equals shared identity. From a scientific perspective, Reality is made of structures of intimate coherence, all the way up and all the way down. **So in order to create a new collective consciousness, in order to create a new collective intelligence, we need a new cultural Democratization of Enlightenment.**

A cultural enlightenment has to be based on a new story, and a new story has to be rooted in the deepest and best sciences that we have, both external and internal knowledge, which becomes the very ground of our self-understanding. And most importantly: *It has to be rooted in the ground of value itself.*

BEING WELCOME IS BEING NEEDED

Let's go back to that home that we were being welcomed to. As we began our conversation, we said that when someone opens the door and welcomes us in and says, "Welcome, welcome," we might not always *feel* welcome. **To begin to truly be welcome, I need to feel and I need to know that I'm inseparable from the Ground of Being.**

We enter into the activities of our life not as something that exhausts us and destroys us, but delighting in creativity as we are manifesting Beauty, Goodness, Truth, and Reality, as we're in the Eros of Creation.

- In order to be welcome in Reality, I not only have to realize my True Self
- I not only have to realize that I'm one with the field of consciousness and desire
- I not only have to realize Einstein's realization that my separate self is an optical delusion of consciousness…

I need to do something else: To really be welcome, I need to realize that Reality needs me.

Imagine you're at that table where you don't quite feel welcome. The hosts are doing their best to welcome you, but it's a little awkward. And then they get a phone call—they answer, their face goes white, a little gasp escapes their mouth, and they say, "Oh my God." They get off the phone and say, "Oh my God, we have this huge emergency. I can't believe that you're here, and it's only you, with your particular set of skills, your set of gifts, and your set of talents—only *you* can help us in this moment." **All of a sudden, you're needed, you're *welcome*, you're fully at home.**

Now your whole body relaxes, you know what to do. It may not appear so dramatically, but you know that you're welcome at the table of Reality. To be fully welcome is to know that:

- You're recognized by Reality.
- You're chosen by Reality.
- You're needed by Reality.
- You're desired by Reality.
- You're adored by Reality.
- You're intended by Reality.

These steps go way beyond Maslow's hierarchy of needs, which outline the needs of the separate self—those are a beautiful, necessary start, but they're not enough. **We need to move beyond survival needs, belonging needs, self-esteem needs, and even self-actualization needs, because those are all interpreted and understood as "deficiency" needs.** These are the needs I have according to win/lose metrics, in rivalrous conflict, useful

139

only for finite games. Those separate-self needs are part of the Success 2.0, win-lose competition:

We have to go deeper—we need to be recognized and be chosen in our uniqueness. **We have a need to be not just loved but *adored* as a unique expression**.

- We have a need *to be recognized* in our uniqueness.
- We have a need *to be chosen* in our uniqueness.
- We have a need *to be desired* in our uniqueness.
- We have a need not just to be loved, but *to be adored* uniquely.
- We have a need *to be intended* by Reality.
- We have a need *to be needed* by Reality.

Those are the six core *Eros needs* that every human being has.

And each need is a right.

Structurally speaking, evolution is love-in-action responding to need. So, my essential needs, my clarified needs, are also my rights!

I have a right to be intended. When I access the nature of Reality, I realize: I didn't decide *when* to be born, I didn't decide *where* to be born, I didn't decide *whom* to be born to. I didn't manifest all of my molecular structure, my atomic structure, my cellular structure, my DNA code. Francis Crick, who first described the complexity of DNA, said it could never have developed naturally, so it must have been seeded by extraterrestrials. He was an atheist, but understood that DNA was a complete impossibility if the universe was random. So he said that aliens must have seeded it—that was his only solution.

I was born into my DNA code. My DNA code welcomes me. **I was intended by Reality uniquely**. That's what *Homo amor* understands.

"I was *intended* by Reality" means that I'm welcome.

"I'm *needed* by Reality" means that I'm welcome.

In our actual experience of uniqueness, we can experience Reality seeing us, recognizing us, and we feel welcome. As we grow reacquainted with this felt sense, knowing deeply that we're held, bathed, and caressed by Reality, literally breathed into existence in every second, we feel adored and needed by Reality—always already welcome.

All of our cells are allured to each other. As electromagnetism, gravitation, and the strong and weak nuclear forces operate in fields of attraction and sustain us every moment, **we feel desired by Reality**. We're all essentially *needed* by Reality. Our individual uniqueness—encoded in our DNA, encoded in our particularities—tells us that we're welcome at the table of Reality. **We're welcome at the table of Reality** not only as True Self, but **as Unique Self. We are needed exactly as we are—with all our shadows, with all our skills—by All-That-Is.**

The experience of being needed is the experience of being welcome, enmeshed in the Field of Value.

THAT WHICH UNITES US IS GREATER THAN THAT WHICH DIVIDES US

The only way to get underneath tribalization and polarization is to understand: *that which unites us is so much greater than that which divides us.* What unites us is that we're all welcome. If there's no welcome home sign in Cosmos, then all our individual welcome home signs are fictions, figments of our imagination. **If we think for a second that there's going to be a world for our grandchildren, that all of our work is actually going to yield fruit without first establishing in the collective psyche and the One Heart of Cosmos, in the One Love, that we're always already totally welcome, that the Mother is screaming *Welcome* every second—then we don't have a chance.**

To be welcome means that I've addressed my six core needs as a human being. I know that I'm intended by Reality. And we know it to be true all the time, in every situation, no matter what.

Without this fundamental understanding, we often say to one person, "You're the person I love. My mother, my father, my husband, my child— you're going to make me feel welcome." It doesn't work. You can't be welcomed in your family if your family is not welcomed by Cosmos. You can't restrict the need to be welcomed to one or two people if we're not all of us always already welcome. Otherwise, you hurt them or they hurt you. Then you try and find another person to welcome you because that didn't work. You can't be welcome anywhere in Cosmos unless there's a welcome home sign in all of Reality, unless there's a Mother. Mother is the ocean, Mother is the inherent goodness of Cosmos.

- Goodness is a welcome home sign. The evolution of goodness is the evolution of my experience in the expansion of that welcome.
- Truth is a welcome home sign.
- Beauty is a welcome home sign.
- Music is a welcome home sign.
- Molecular biology is a welcome home sign.
- The gorgeousness of advanced calculus and the infinite elegance and erotic play of mathematics—aligned with both the human mind and the Cosmos—are welcome home signs of Cosmos.
- Science itself is a welcome home sign.

That there absolutely is a welcome home sign everywhere, that we're always welcome, is what our children need to understand—the child in us as well, not just our biological children.

That which unites us is so much greater than that which divides us. That's the beginning of the experience of *Homo amor*.

3.5

INTRODUCTION TO GENESIS 29: THE BIRTH OF *HOMO AMOR*

In order to unite Reality, in order to create a larger and greater union, we need to integrate all the wisdom streams, each of which has its own beautiful welcome home sign. We need the traditional sacred texts, the sacred texts of science, of modernity, of existentialism, and the sacred texts of postmodernity. Each of these sacred texts speaks to a different, important dimension of value.

Currently, seventy percent of the world **lives in relationship to some sacred text**. But we in the West are largely split off from them. Sacred texts have dimensions that are not sacred, that human consciousness in its shadow form overtook and corrupted.

At its core, sacred text embodies the deepest experience of Eros which pours through and transmits Goodness, Truth, and Beauty—and speaks in larger mystical mythologies.

They hold us and give us a way to orient ourselves in our Reality and create a shared language. We need to create a shared language by integrating sacred texts from all of the different dimensions of history, **letting them inform and create us**. Today, we live in a world alienated from the sacred, from the deepest aspects of science and Spirit. We're going to now look at a sacred text of Spirit called Genesis.

We've talked about the four Big Bangs: first matter appears; then matter triumphs in life, and the biosphere emerges; then life triumphs as the self-reflective human mind, the noosphere, the thinking realm of culture. Matter-life-culture: Those are the first three Big Bangs. But mind and culture continue to evolve. The notion that *Homo sapiens* is going to remain as *Homo sapiens* violates the structure of evolution. **Evolution always keeps evolving.**

There's a moment in which we either crash into our planetary boundaries because evolution has stopped, stalled, or meandered, or the evolution of love continues and *Homo sapiens* explodes into the next level of humanity: what we are calling *Homo amor*. That process began with da Vinci in the Renaissance, some 300 or 400 years ago—exterior technologies kept developing and interior technologies collapsed on themselves. *Our contemporary interior technologies can't deal with Reality:*

- We can't deal with a broken information ecology.
- We can't deal with artificial intelligence.
- We can't deal with machine learning.
- We can't deal with a world in which jobs are rapidly going to disappear.
- We can't deal with eight billion people.
- We can't deal with viruses transmitted in a non-local world.

We can't deal with the world that's alienated from a Universal Grammar of Value, where we have eight billion separate cells in rivalrous conflict, or organized into larger competing nations. That's a recipe for total destruction, and arguably what's generated the many forms of existential risk.

Researchers at Oxford's Future of Humanity Institute, like Toby Ord in his book *The Precipice*, give us a fifty percent chance of making it through the next five hundred years.

What do we do? We cannot go to despair. We don't look down—we look up. **We're pressed into service. The second shock of existence—our realization of the potential for existential and catastrophic risk—instead exhilarates us, invites us to participate as part of evolution.**

THE HISTORICAL BIRTH OF THE IDEA OF HOMO AMOR

One of the first moments in history when the idea of *Homo amor*, the New Human and the New Humanity, broke forth, was in the emergent relationship between the father and daughter. There is a moment in history when the daughter became not a potential mate for the father—the object of his desire—but the subject of his love and protection. This is not the fully realized *Homo amor* that integrates evolutionary science, molecular physics, mysticism, feminism, postmodern theory, and all the rest, but an early realization that the human being can be more, and can actually become *Homo amor*.

Early *Homo amor* has Eastern and Western expressions. Let's explore the Western lens, and the mythic idea of the Christ Child, which is so central to the *Da Vinci Code*. Jesus, who's born as this Christ Child, traces his lineage back to King David in Jerusalem. David's son was Solomon, who built the temple in Jerusalem, where the two cherubs above the Ark of the Covenant are passionately intertwined—the voice of meaning and Spirit comes from the space between the two cherubs.

David and Solomon trace their lineage back not to Jacob, but to Judah, and the well-known Lion of Judah symbol is related to the Wisdom of Solomon. **Judah is a figure who breaks through in human history—the first emergence of what's later going to be called "Messiah."**

In the fundamentalist religions, messiah refers to only one human being, someone like Jesus or David or Solomon, who is no longer just *Homo sapiens* but someone who is lived as love. Jesus, for example, offers this new teaching on love because he's an early expression of *Homo amor*. The original intention of the idea of messiah is not that there's one person who's the messiah, but that Jesus, Mary—his mother—and Mary Magdalene, his partner, are actually all representative of a New Human and a New Humanity.

Judah represents one of the earliest Western expressions of the notion of Enlightenment, wherein the goal of Reality is not merely to have one person (Judah, David, Solomon, Jesus, etc.) live as expansive love. Rather, it's the realization that none are separate from Spirit, **that in some sense we are all of us Mother and Son; Father, Son and Holy Ghost; Infinite and finite; Divinity and humanity**—as Dante says, "we're all baby-faced divines."

We're not just part of the field of eternal being, we're also the field of human becoming, propelled collectively by the evolutionary impulse itself.

We are evolutionary love personified. This knowing is sourced in Judah. He's arguably the first *Homo amor* figure in the West, a key source of this evolutionary development in human history. But we have to understand how *Homo amor* is born: the experience of being welcome, the experience of the Mother, all of the welcome signs in Cosmos.

As we said before, **whether or not you're able to be lived as love in the best sense comes from your experience of the universe mediated by your mother**. At the cutting edge of attachment theory, there's a realization that the mother is much bigger than the biological mother, much closer to what we talked about earlier, the "welcome home" sign in Cosmos.

We're overcoming the alienation between the sciences and the humanities, making them intimate with each other again. Mathematics is music, and music is mathematics.

We're recovering *Homo amor*—not as an individual person but as a Democratization of Enlightenment, of sanity, for every human being.

Enlightenment is sanity. And sanity is not the province of the elite, but the province of every human being.

THE CHARACTERS IN GENESIS 29

Let's explore chapter 29 of the Book of Genesis: Abraham and his wife, Sarah, are the first patriarch and first matriarch in the great Genesis story. They have two children, Ishmael and Isaac. Isaac receives the family business, while Ishmael goes off to create another world of spirit. They split into two worlds.

Isaac has two kids, Jacob and Esau. Even though Isaac wanted to give the family business to Esau, Jacob receives the blessing, because his mother, Rebecca, says, "Listen to me: get dressed up like your brother Esau in hairy clothes using animal skins and deceive your father. He doesn't understand his children. Esau is not the guy to carry on this blessing, you need to carry on this blessing. Deceive your father for the sake of the greater good and get the blessing."

Jacob is initially hesitant, but agrees in the end. His father Isaac gives him the blessing. When Esau hears about this, he is totally devastated and wants to kill his brother. Rebecca then advises Jacob to leave and go to his uncle, Laban, in a place called Paddan-aram—*aram* means deception. She's effectively saying, "go to the place of deception," because Jacob has become a deceiver.

Laban has two daughters, Rachel and Leah. When Jacob arrives, he falls in love with Rachel, so Laban says, "Work for me for seven years, and I'll give you my daughter, Rachel, as your wife." Jacob says, "Wonderful." So he works for seven years, and then, as was the custom at the time, the bride is heavily cloaked and veiled. Jacob comes to the wedding, the bride is cloaked and veiled, and afterwards they go into a dark room. They make love the first time, but they don't even see each other. He wakes up in the morning, and behold... it's Leah, the older sister! Jacob, who deceived his father and took the blessing, is now deceived.

Then the text describes the birth of the first four children of Leah and Jacob: Reuben, Simon, Levi, and Judah. Verse 25 reads:

> *It was in the morning and Jacob opens his eyes, and it is Leah. Jacob says to Laban, "What have you done to me? I've worked for Rachel who I was in love with, why have you deceived me?"*

Verse 26:

> *Laban answers, "We don't do this in our place, to give the younger before the older. Work for another seven years."*

What happened that night? When Leah shows up instead of Rachel, it's very clear Leah had to participate in the deception. Leah has a sister named Rachel, with whom Jacob has fallen in love, and yet Leah agrees to participate in the deception of Jacob. Rachel is beautiful, and Leah is more plain, but she is also a powerful, mystical/mythical figure. Somehow she agrees to participate in this deception. Clearly something is happening here.

This is the mystical moment in Western history in which the Da Vinci Code really starts, the pivotal story that is going to yield Mary Magdalene, the Christ Child, and Homo amor, the story of the New Human.

The entire notion of progress in history and the notion that humanity can transform comes from this mystical text.

WHY DID LEAH (YOU) AGREE TO DECEIVE JACOB?

The way the interior scientists read it is to step into it. Become Leah. *You are Leah.* Place yourself in her position. Why did you deceive Jacob? Why did you agree to participate in that deception?

Perhaps you imagine that you're really ugly and if you don't sneak in front of the line before Rachel, who's not going to have a problem finding a husband, you'll be alone forever. You'll die alone in a cold room and never have kids. Similarly, you were resentful of Rachel always getting all the attention and she can have all the men she wants. Deceiving Jacob is your only shot at it. This is a win-lose metric.

Or perhaps you did it to honor your father. You were caught in the patriarchal structures of society, and couldn't fully become the woman you wanted to be. You couldn't make the choices you wanted to make because your father demanded that you be a particular way. So you betrayed your sister to honor the father.

Or perhaps it's your right as the eldest daughter, and you don't care about Rachel. You're going to claim your birthright. Sometimes life hurts. Are you willing to claim your right even if it hurts?

Perhaps you live according to the structures of society and are not fully responsible for your decisions. You can't help it—you've got to do what has to be done.

Or perhaps you married Jacob in the darkness because you had a sense in your body that you would be the mother of the future. You had a sense of destiny that was so strong that you had to override any other value you had—you had to override honesty, integrity, loyalty, and the love of your sister because destiny is calling you.

Perhaps you were so in love with him, so you told your dad you had to marry him and he did it for you. He somehow gave you the chance because you were his favorite child, and we know the power a child has to manipulate his or her parents. You knew how to manipulate your dad into becoming your partner in deception. Don't daughters know how to use their dads?

Or perhaps you thought you had one choice: you could be exiled from your parents and all sustenance and support, or you could be exiled from your sister. You chose the easier exile. We have to make hard choices in life. We have to survive. Rather than being exiled from your job, family, society, you betrayed your sister! We've all fucked over our siblings to get ahead, taken the guy, deceived them in some way, because we can't be exiled from the entire structure of society. We can't step in and really meet our greatness. We need to be held in our social structures and make sure that our parents and our friends all think we're appropriate and good. Existential risk? We don't have time for that.

Or perhaps it's because you believe that Rachel loves herself too much, and that you'd actually be a much better mother. You know she's not going to do as good a job as you. You're a good person and you deserve it.

Or perhaps it's because when you saw Jacob look at Rachel, you wanted him right then, from the very start. You wanted to be desired in that way. You were dying to be that woman the eyes of men feast upon. You wanted to have that body, to be that woman who walked into the room and who all eyes turned towards. There's an entire cosmetics industry devoted to trying to convince women that they can be that woman. Perhaps you're standing for all women who want to be desired, not just the ostensibly beautiful ones.

CONTEMPLATION EXERCISE:
LEAH IN THE DARKNESS

Place yourself in the position of Leah here. How many of us recognize that we've done our version of "marrying Jacob in the darkness," betrayed someone because we had no choice, because we couldn't help ourselves, because we didn't want to die alone and lonely? Because we were jealous? Because of society?

What would it be like to act in this way? What are the reasons you might do so? Can you imagine the unconscious or cultural forces driving you?

Can you imagine what it might be like not to feel fundamentally welcome in Cosmos?

Are you relying on only one person for that, doing everything in your power to retain that narrow sense of welcome?

Are there situations in your life, minor or major, where you've acted in similar ways? Can you see the way that darkness governs aspects of our lives?

Write it all out in your journal—be honest, let go, and prepare the way for the transformations to come.

MARRYING IN THE DARKNESS = RIVALROUS CONFLICT BASED ON WIN-LOSE METRICS

Leah marries Jacob in the darkness. We've all done similar things in our lives. We all now realize we've been *Homo sapiens.* In this archetypal story, you married Jacob in the darkness. We've all married Jacob in the darkness, so to speak, in some way.

What happens when it doesn't work, when Jacob does not intend you? You don't feel so good. The basic human needs—*to be intended, to be chosen, to be recognized, to be desired, to be adored, and to be needed*—are not at all addressed by Jacob. He's not taking walks with you, he's not desiring you, nor does he give any sense that he needs you. He's certainly not adoring you. What do you do?

151

You make the classic move: you have a child—that'll fix everything for sure. How many recognize that move in culture? We all know that move. The child might be a creative project or a business project. But often it's an actual child. Look what happens in Verse 32.

> *God saw that Leah was hated and God opened her womb. And she gave birth to a child, and she called the child Reuben because she said, "God has seen my misery, and maybe now my husband will love me."*

Reuben means: *God saw I was miserable.* I was suffering, but maybe now that I have a child, I will be the cause of love. It's a pretty bad name to receive. Instead of naming her child Jack or Tom, she names her kid, *God saw my affliction so maybe now my husband will love me.*

Reuben means God saw I'm experiencing my misery, maybe my husband will love me and have dinner with me. I'm experiencing my misery, maybe my husband will love me and take me out. I'm experiencing my misery, maybe my husband will love me and remember my birthday.

Reuben is going to internalize his mother's degradation later in the Book of Genesis. His life is going to crash because he hasn't been received or welcomed by the mother. He's a mere object in his mother's ploy, in her win-lose calculation to achieve Jacob's love.

This doesn't work out, so in Verse 33 she gives birth to another child, Simeon, which essentially means, *God saw that I was hated.* So *God saw that I was miserable* has a brother named *God saw that I was hated.* It's a long story, but he eventually becomes a massive zealot, and participates in a massacre in Chapter 34, in the town of Shechem. He certainly wasn't received by his mother.

And then she has another kid, Verse 34. Third time's a charm, right? She said, "Now at last my husband will become attached to me, because I have borne him three sons." The name of the new kid is Levi, or *maybe this time my husband will love me and take walks with me.* And children internalize everything. Much of the rest of the Book of Genesis traces the story of

Homo sapiens. **What's going to happen to Reuben, Simon, and Levi, who've all internalized their mother's degradation, who've internalized their mother's frustration, who've internalized their fathers un-love?**

Leah is stuck. She married Jacob in the darkness in order to feel welcome; and then when she doesn't feel welcome, she starts having kids. If I don't have Jacob, Leah says, then I'm not welcome in the Cosmos. Her "welcome home" sign in the Cosmos is in her gestalt, with one word written on it: Jacob.

If your "welcome home" sign has only one name on it, you will kill, murder, and steal. You might not do it overtly, you might betray people, deceive them or undermine them. You might be a silent assassin, a silent deceiver, a silent murderer. But you're always going to make sure that your welcome home sign, which is your success, is there—whatever it looks like.

It's not that you're not a good person. You're a good woman, you're a good guy, you do nice things. **But what's really driving you, the animating story of your life, is the generator function of existential risk: rivalrous conflict based on win-lose metrics.** You marry Jacob in the darkness because your welcome home sign, the way you understand it, is rivalrous conflict based on win-lose metrics.

DEMOCRATIZATION OF ENLIGHTENMENT

How does *Homo sapiens* become *Homo amor*? When I say *Homo amor* is about to be born, we're not there yet, but at the first sighting. *Homo amor* has to include all of premodern, modern, and postmodern advances. We have to include everything, but the first intimation of the possibility of a New Human and a New Humanity—which the great traditions call Messiah— limit *Homo amor* to one person, Jesus or David or Solomon, or the guru.

It's why we reject the guru principle. Instead, we need a full *Democratization of Enlightenment*. We're all able to access Enlightenment—not just the guru.

---

*We need to be able to directly access Homo amor living and breathing as us, as **we're lived as love**.*

How does it happen? Let's take a look at an unbelievable text, Verse 35 of Genesis 29.

The verse says: *And she gives birth again and she gives birth to a son*, and this is Leah's fourth son and she says *this time I embrace, I acknowledge, I'm filled with gratitude, I'm living in the presence of God. She called him Judah.* The word this time comes from *odeh*, which means I acknowledge, I self-recognize. **Judah means *self-recognition*.**

3.6

LEAH'S BREAKTHROUGH: TOWARDS HOMO AMOR, LIVING AS LOVE

Leah's lost in win-lose metrics and then something happens, and she is able to break the patterns of her past. People are supposedly unchangeable, so what happened? She was able to access some other dimension of her being by giving birth to a fourth child. She was supposed to only have three. Jacob has four wives, and there are twelve tribes. Four times three equals twelve, so each wife should have had only three.

But Leah had four—this is a big surprise.

Somehow there's a shocking self-recognition. Judah is born, the ancestor of David and Solomon—but not a biological ancestor. In the Genesis text, he's a lineage ancestor. He's of the soul root, he's the quality of Jesus, he's the quality of David, he's the quality of Solomon, he represents the Cherubs above the Ark.

Judah is born in this moment, and he gives birth to something new. What happens in this moment that births Judah? It was Leah who calls him forth. And remember, *we are all Leah*—we've all acted in darkness, and we're all able to shift and transform in this way.

So again, place yourself in Leah's position, feel deep into her life—don't merely think about this but feel it in your story. I am Leah, you are Leah, we are all Leah. The way the interior scientists say it is "**I participate in Leah-ness.**" This is one of the deepest ways that mystics used to study the sacred texts.

WHAT HAPPENED TO LEAH?

So Leah, what happened? How did you change? How did you reverse the pattern? How did you stop naming your kids things like, "I saw I was hated and my husband wouldn't take walks with me"? All of a sudden you named your kid *Here I am in the presence of the Divine.* What happened? What was your breakthrough? How were you able, all of a sudden, to experience your own "enoughness" so that you could give birth to this lineage of love, which would produce Jesus and Magdalene. Ultimately in the twenty-first century, this would produce the Democratization of Enlightenment, the new collective intelligence, *the new Dharma,* the emergence of a new shared grammar of evolving and eternal value in which we're all lived as love.

> *Perhaps after all this searching outside yourself to find value and meaning, you paused and stopped and listened and looked inside and opened up your ears. What you heard was, "I am Love." You looked around, and there was some place where you couldn't feel your own enoughness. Then there was a moment where something changed, and **all of a sudden you realized "yes, I'm Enough, I am Lived as Love"—that's what matters and that's what's important and that's what's real.***

> *Or perhaps you just felt your heart open right up. Perhaps you felt something move within, something new. Perhaps you felt the birth of something new within you that changed the inexorable pattern of your life. The Cosmos moved in you, a breaking open, a breaking out, and breaking through, something totally unexpected, completely joyous, amazing, a Joy beyond Joy.*

Or perhaps, all of a sudden you somehow felt that you weren't just small Leah in some little life just trying to get by. Something deep opened up. Maybe you were chanting, or praying, or reading, desperate in the middle of the night, maybe you were taking a walk in nature seeking answers, maybe doing psilocybin, studying philosophy, meditating in a cave, and **all of a sudden you were able to see the whole picture and all of a sudden the whole picture opened up in you and something larger was born for the first time.** *You felt the Cosmos in you, and you were no longer just a separate self. You could feel something much bigger moving in and through you.*

Or perhaps you saw yourself as completely new: beautiful, radiant, grand, a part of all that is. And from there, you could finally stand up. Separate self is an optical delusion of consciousness—and **you actually realized the interconnectivity of the whole thing moving through you, realizing that you're an utterly unique node of beauty and love of the interconnected, Intimate Universe, unlike any other.** *You can now stand in the presence of Reality, in the presence of God.*

Or perhaps you gave up. You finally surrendered, totally and deeply. Beat down by the course of your life you miraculously realized, albeit with some great difficulty, that your struggles against what you had been served in life were all in vain. So you gave up. **When you stopped the fight, when you stopped pressing against all of Reality,** *desperately trying to marry Jacob in the darkness, something happened and something shifted. And at that exact moment, you were filled with deep realization and gratitude.*

Or perhaps the pain became so great from all the betrayal, the denial, and the hate, and you couldn't turn anywhere. So much betrayal and so much rivalry, and you just got stuck. You were stuck for so long that suddenly—you have no idea exactly what happened—the heavens broke through.

Or perhaps deep down you just knew there had to be more to life than perpetuating the same win-lose metrics for the next ten generations through your children. There was a different way. At a certain point you realized that it simply had to change. So you opened up to new possibilities. It was a breakthrough from Homo sapiens to Homo amor.

Or perhaps you finally felt, you finally knew, that you deserved to receive life fully. And you knew that you wouldn't get it by marrying Jacob in the darkness, or through passing down trauma to your children. You realized that you deserve to receive life fully.

Or perhaps you saw your sister's struggle in a new way and it broke your heart open. You were able for the first time in your life to feel someone who wasn't you. Sometimes we can go through our whole lives unable to truly feel others. It's one of the hardest things in the world to feel another person like you feel yourself. That's Homo amor.

CONTEMPLATION EXERCISE:
LEAH BECOMES HOMO AMOR

Place yourself in Leah's position, after all the betrayal and deception, after all the victim mentality, after all the failed attempts to have your needs met, after all the failed attempts to feel welcome in Cosmos.

Think about your own life—make it personal. What changed? What shifted? What could have caused the transformation? In your journal write out the details of your own birth of Homo amor.

Have there been other moments in your life, minor or major, where something has broken through, where a new felt sense or a new way of being—previously unimaginable—emerged, or became your new embodied perspective? What happened, what were the details? Remembering these moments, however small, is incredibly important for integrating any insights, and deepening the transformation into Homo amor in your own life.

3.7

JUDAH BECOMES LEAH'S WELCOME HOME SIGN IN COSMOS

Judah is the beginning of *Homo amor*: the breakthrough moment when *Homo sapiens*—the Leah who marries Jacob in the darkness—becomes *Homo amor* and births Judah. Judah is the beginning of the Messiah energy in Western history. That's where Mary Magdalene comes from. That's where Christ comes from. That's where the African-American gospel comes from. That's the moment of breakthrough.

The actual phrase in the breakthrough moment is when Leah says: "this time, *odeh et Adonai*." *Odeh* means. "I say thank you." **This time I say thank you to God, and I hear God or Reality replying, "you're welcome."** That's the story. *Odeh,* " thank you," and Reality says "you're welcome."

I feel welcome before the Divine.

I feel like I'm enough.

I feel like I have a home.

Every time she was holding Reuben, who would she see when she looked down? She would see Jacob and say: *God knows that I'm in misery.* Poor kid. Then when she was looking down at baby Simeon in her arms, who did

159

she see? She saw Jacob and said, *God knew that I was hated*. Then she had her third child Levi in her arms, and who did she see? She saw Jacob and said, *maybe my man will love me now*. Every parent here who educates their child into such narrow win-lose metrics—every educator, every teacher, and every facilitator who educates their child into "marrying Jacob in the darkness"—is naming their child, regardless of whatever specific name we give them: *God saw that I was hated*.

That's what C.S. Lewis writes about in *The Abolition of Man*: When we condition a child to play by win-lose metrics, they only have value if they've produced in a certain way, and get paid in a certain way within the structure of a particular industrial society—without that, they have no value. We're looking at our children and saying, "Hello *God saw that I was hated*, I'm going to introduce you into this win-lose metrics, and unfortunately I'm going to be depressed my whole life. I'm going to occasionally get away for a good vacation, but basically I'm going to burn out. And I have no choice but to raise you to be successful and burn out just like me."

But then something new happens. Leah has a fourth child—and this is the quality of surprise, the quality of *something that I couldn't imagine happening*. I was sure I couldn't come through this. I was sure I'd always be in the same pattern of life. I was only supposed to have three children—and all of a sudden I have four. **I'm radically surprised, so I allow myself to be surprised—for the first time, my eyes are open, and I have seen the glory.**

All our eyes have to open. We have to feel this, and go through a mystical transfiguration in this very moment. What needs to happen is to look down at the baby in our arms and to see who? When she looks down at Judah, who does she see? She sees Judah. Absolutely. For the first time she looks at the baby and she sees Judah and she feeds Judah, her eyes open. My eyes have seen the glory of the coming of the Lord—and the name of the glory is Judah.

3.8

THE BIRTH OF OUTRAGEOUS LOVE AS A PERCEPTION

This transformation of Leah into *Homo amor* means: I'm a lover. And to be a lover is *to see with evolutionary eyes, with God's eyes.* *Homo amor* means that when I see you, I'm actually seeing YOU. I'm not seeing a means for me to succeed in my win-lose metrics. Do you know how rarely we're actually seen by someone? To be a lover is "to have eyes to see." For *Homo amor*, love at its core is not merely an emotion. When I was with the Dalai Lama, he got very excited when I said to him, **"In our lineage, love is not an emotion—it's a perception."**

To be a lover is to see infinite beauty. Love is a Unique Self-perception. Leah sees Judah, and when I'm seen as Judah I become Messiah. That's what it means. *Homo amor* means we move beyond *Homo sapiens*, and we can literally see each other and say, "Behold, you're beautiful, Beloved. Behold."

In the way we do it, we say "thank you." When we say thank you, we hear the Universe, the ocean, the Mother reply: "you're welcome." We want to practice around the world, wherever we are on the path, seeing each other with God's eyes, as *Homo amor*, as mad lovers.

SHORT INTRODUCTION TO CERTAINTY

Certainty does not mean knowing that something is true, that my model is true, that my scientific dogma or my religious dogma is true. **Certainty means knowing *I am true*—that's my core certainty of being**. My core certainty of being is—*"I am true, I'm enough, I'm welcome in the Cosmos."* So the practice is to gather the welcome home signs in Cosmos because they're all over the place, to look at my Beloved and say, for the first time, in the words of Emily Dickinson, oh my God:

> *Not revelation—'tis—that waits,*
> *But my unfurnished eyes.*

I can see clearly now. I can see you. *Behold, you are beautiful, Beloved.* These are the words of *Homo amor*, Solomon, who is from the Judah tradition. Solomon built the Temple with the cherubs above the ark, and he writes to all of us.

Behold, you are beautiful, Beloved.

HOMO AMOR REALIZES OUR LOVE LISTS ARE TOO SHORT

Homo amor knows and realizes "my love lists are too short." It's not enough for me just to love my immediate family, or the people in my tribe.

I can't just move from egocentric to ethnocentric intimacy, and stop at, "I love my tribe, I'm willing to die for my tribe." That's not enough. I've got to love big, not just by abstractly loving the "whole world." *I must be willing to fall in love with specific, real people all the time.* This doesn't mean romantic love, or moving in together. Romantic love is just one beautiful dimension of love. ***Homo amor* means: I'm literally willing to open my heart and fall in love with an idea, even though it's not my own. I'm willing to fall in love with Beauty, with Goodness, with Truth.**

162

I'm willing to fall madly in love with YOU, feeling this love pulsing in my being, feeling your pain, your sorrow, your greatness. It's why we call Love "Outrageous." It's a raging love—an Outrageous Love.

Most of us only feel that love for a short time, and for only one person—maybe two. But that's not how we want to live our lives. For *Homo amor*, that's how we live—all the time. I fall in love with new ideas, with new people, with new parts of my Beloved, with the split off parts of myself. **Nothing's outside the circle. That's *Homo amor*.** There's no part of myself I'm not going to fall in love with.

I'm in love with ALL of myself, and I'm in love with ALL of you.

We're going to transmute and hold all of it, and each other. Any problem or awkwardness that arises—we love each other right through and beyond them to the other side. *We can love each other madly. We're actually in love.* The desire of the Infinite Intimate that manifested Cosmos lives in us, pulses in us.

I am evolution, we are evolution. That's the realization of *Homo amor*. I'm the personal face of the throbbing, dripping, tumescent, alive, pulsating, evolutionary impulse—I am madly in love with Reality, and with you. We can absolutely love more than one person—in fact, it's our responsibility to do so. And once again, this doesn't mean I'm going to marry or live with ten people. We're not doing ordinary love here. No, this is mad love, Outrageous Love.

To be *Homo amor* is to viscerally feel the mad love of Cosmos pulsing alive in us...

CHAPTER 4

THE DANCE BETWEEN CERTAINTY AND UNCERTAINTY

4.1

PRAYER: OPENING AGAIN TO LOVE

Whenever new space opens up, there's always a play between the light and the vessel. Whenever we expand and deepen, we work with the vessels. And of course, it always expresses itself physically in some way. We don't get to articulate a new story that's all sweetness and light; it is quite demanding.

So in order to expand our vessels, our hearts and our bodies, and find our way through any contractions, let's revisit our prayer by Foreigner, again but as if for the first time. We open the space of prayer, reaching, opening to the love that lies at the source of everything—a*nd we stake our entire lives on it.*

PRAYER: "I WANT KNOW WHAT LOVE IS," FOREIGNER

We're on the inside, with full heart, like we've never prayed before. Feel free to listen to this song, to this prayer—and sing and dance along to it. Into the Silence of Presence, in the space between the breaths.

In my life, there's been heartache and pain
I don't know if I can face it again
Can't stop now, I've traveled so far
To change this lonely life

I wanna know what love is
I want you to show me
I wanna feel what love is
I know you can show me

4.2

RECAPITULATION & REVIEW

FROM PRE-TRAGIC TO TRAGIC

In the first chapter we moved through a potential near-future scenario, through the 2020s, 2030s, 2040s, and 2050s, to get a first-person experience of what civilizational collapse could look like. We stepped into the second shock of existence, from the pandemic shocks of the 2020s, to the climate shocks of the 2030s, to the ecosystem shocks of the 2040s, and then potential civilizational collapse in the 2050s. This was a speculative prediction, based on trends, with an enormous amount of complex information and data underlying it. But this was not a prophecy— and certainly not a self-fulfilling prophecy. Quite the opposite. **We were practicing being willing to not look away**. As Robert Jay Lifton says, we must face Apocalypse, which is more real now than it has ever been in human history.

Instead of looking away, we traced the relationship between the exponential and the existential, and how exponential technology creates existential risk—not because of its existence per se, but because of the matrix in which it plays, and from which it arises.

FROM TRAGIC TO POST-TRAGIC

After walking through the pre-tragic to the tragic, we made some initial moves towards the post-tragic. We walked through nine or ten dramatic steps, each one critical, to recalibrate consciousness and culture itself. We explored a radical sense of possibility, understanding what Spirit is, what love is: **Love is the Possibility of Possibility.**

Love is not merely an ordinary human experience, accidentally generated in a random Cosmos, but the heart of existence itself, the Eros that "moves the sun and other stars," that animates Reality, all the way down and all the way up the evolutionary chain.

It's the single-most important force in our lives because we *participate* in Cosmos, the same Cosmos that allures subatomic particles to form larger wholes, which move separate parts into larger wholes, all the way up the evolutionary chain, moving us to form the larger wholes in our lives, culminating in our becoming *Homo amor.*

Homo amor is not omniscient or omnipotent, but omni-considerate— but *Homo amor* always moves for the sake of the whole. We step out of our own narcissism, and feel the whole moving in us. *We understand that we are needed by the whole, that we each have a gift to give that serves not only our own individual transformations, but the transformation of the whole thing.*

That's the beginning of the experience of *Homo amor.*

THE HIGHEST LEVEL OF PLEASURE IS THE POWER TO AFFECT THE WHOLE THING—FOR THE GOOD

In the 2020 Eros Mystery School, we explored pleasure and Eros as the source of ethics, expanding on what pleasure commonly means, and we looked at six levels of pleasure.[10] Each level has its own principles at play, and there is no rate of exchange between any level of pleasure. For example, all the pleasure of level one couldn't get you any of level two's pleasure. And all of level two couldn't get you any of level three, and so on—but subsequent levels included all previous levels.

The sixth level of pleasure is the pleasure of power. We have to be "power-hungry." We must desire power—not the power of the separate-self ego desiring to aggrandize itself in a hopeless and pathetic endeavor—but the genuine power of the evolutionary impulse moving through us, the power of impacting ever wider circles of influence.

When he was president, Barack Obama was happy when he woke up in the morning because he had power. He ran for president because he was attracted and allured by pleasure, but what pleasure? *The pleasure of power.* You don't run for president unless you can feel the pleasure of power for the sake of the whole—the highest level of pleasure is power.

In this new worldview, rooted deeply in the sciences, **Reality exists for the sake of pleasure**. As evolutionary scientist Kathy Pell Kaufman writes, "Evolution evolves because it feels good." Even at the level of quarks, there's a kind of quantum "hedonism." **There's an Eros, a sense of attraction and allurement that animates everything.** Alfred North Whitehead's key notions center around the desire or the pleasure inherent in Reality—or what he called the "appetition" of Cosmos. One of the most important Whitehead scholars, David Ray Griffin, noticed this, and we can find it everywhere in Whitehead's writing.

---

[10] See the forthcoming book, *Pleasure as Ethics,* as well as *"Ten Voices, Twenty-one Principles, Six Levels,"* a chapter in the volume, *CosmoErotic Humanism.*

Let's quickly review the principles of pleasure.

First, Reality is for pleasure.

Next, the highest level of pleasure is the pleasure of power, the pleasure of transformation.

Finally, this highest level of power, which transforms the whole, is the power of *self-transformation*, knowing that my own transformation transforms the whole thing. It's the knowledge that evolution lives in me, and that I live in evolution, that I am a unique incarnation of the evolutionary impulse, that all lives in me and I live in all, that my transformation transforms the whole thing.

As we move from *Homo sapiens* to *Homo amor*, becoming part of the New Human and the New Humanity, then we respond directly to existential risk in the most powerful way we can.

Da Vinci's beautiful and necessary articulation of a new vision of the human being, a new universe story, took us into modernity, but the weaknesses in that plotline brought us face to face with our planetary boundaries, with extraction models, and with growth curves that fall off, as the Club of Rome pointed out in *The Limits to Growth*, in the early 1970s. We're once again at a moment when the exponential leaps to the existential, where we need to tell the story again, but this time better than it's ever been told.

The good news is: **this is not some wild and blind ambition, but the inherent movement of Cosmos itself:** the Third Big Bang, when life becomes self-reflective mind, naturally moves to the Fourth Big Bang—the emergence of *Homo amor*.

BEING WELCOME IN COSMOS: THE EXPERIENCE OF *HOMO AMOR*

The core experience of *Homo amor* is the gnosis of always feeling profoundly welcome in the Cosmos. So as we make this evolutionary shift, the most important question in the world is: do I know that I am always already welcome in the Cosmos?

We pointed towards "welcome home signs," because welcome means *welcome home*. But are we actually able to see the welcome home signs everywhere around us in Reality? If there's no welcome home sign in the Cosmos, then there would be no welcome home signs in your life. And you can't create contrived welcome home signs, and hope to handle your life while dissociating from Reality. You must be unwilling to turn away from the suffering of the world, which means gradually becoming increasingly omni-considerate for the sake of the whole.

The experience of *Homo amor* is: I'm aware, I feel the Cosmos moving in me. I'm not just an egocentric, ethnocentric lover, I'm a worldcentric, even cosmocentric, omni-considerate, intimate human being: I feel all animals, all plants, all human beings, the whole planet.

To have this experience of being alive as *Homo amor*, I've got to experience a new universe story, understanding that Reality is not random, not "some tale told by an idiot, full of sound and fury, signifying nothing," as Shakespeare wrote. Instead, we know the Cosmos to be gorgeously coherent, or as Richard Feynman said, strangely, gorgeously, utterly waiting and welcoming us in a fundamental way. From the subatomic level all the way up, each and every level is in intimate coherence with the others.

THE MOTHER SAYS, "WELCOME HOME"

In this way, we know we're welcome in the Cosmos, we begin to understand this sense of what we call the Mother. This is not your biological mother, although the human mother at her best can mediate or represent or embody the Great Mother.

Attachment theory says that if you don't experience some amount of deep and profound love early on from your mother, your life is going to go off the rails in some way. Even though, from a neo-Darwinian perspective, you've got food and shelter and everything you *physically* need, if there's some violation, or the love generally fails to hold you in a secure way, then your life will be very difficult until you find the Great Mother, the true Welcome.

This is what attachment theory doesn't understand—it's not just about your mom; it's about the Mother. The way you get your life back on track is through the Mother. **The Mother *is* welcome. The human mother does her best as she welcomes her child into Reality. She says, "Welcome home. It's good that you're here."** She looks at the child and she *sees* the child.

The existentialists got this, they understood this. Their conclusions were wrong, but they understood that if there's no welcome home sign in Cosmos, there's no welcome home sign in your life. And if there's no mother in Cosmos, then then there's no Mother in your life. We talked about *The Stranger,* by Camus, which opens with something like, "Mother died today, or was it yesterday? And does it really matter?" Camus is saying: *I can't find a welcome home sign. There's no Mother. I'm not held and so Mother doesn't matter.*

To really understand our great project together—the Great Library has to include movies and media and podcasts and books, with many people participating and reminding everyone that **we are welcome (home) in Cosmos.**

After the great, and somewhat necessary, deconstructive project that tore down all the welcome home signs, we're now beginning the great **reconstructive project**, by hanging welcome home signs all over Cosmos, with the understanding that Goodness to be one kind of welcome home sign, Truth is another, and Beauty another one as well. We realize:

- **Goodness**—kindness and care are everywhere—*I'm welcome.*
- **Truth**—as seen in mathematics—*I'm welcome.*
- **Beauty**—color and light is a welcome home sign—*I'm welcome.*

It can be seen in nature, as well. The ocean is a common welcome home sign, for example.

One of the texts in the original literature of the Hebrew wisdom interior sciences called divinity *El Shaddai*, which means the breast. One of the names of God is the breast. Why are we allured to breasts (both men and women)? The image of the breast says: **the Cosmos is good—*we're welcome here.*** Skin is also a welcome home sign in Cosmos. These are all welcome home signs in Cosmos.

4.3

THE MOTHER AND WELCOME COME TOGETHER IN GENESIS 29

If I don't feel that I'm truly welcome, then every interaction I have will be some subtle or not-so-subtle form of manipulation—because everything I do is simply trying to get me back to feeling welcome. And if I don't realize I'm already welcome, I can't simply bracket myself and emerge as *Homo amor*—**so if I've lost the experience of feeling welcome, I must get it back again.**

Genesis 29 is the story of the birth of Judah, the ancestor of David, the father of Solomon who built the temple in Jerusalem. In the Christian story, Judah is the lineage ancestor of Jesus and Mary, figures who represent the notion of transformation. They are messianic figures, and Messiah means to step into history, into story, to shift things. The notion of Messiah, which exists in different forms in all the great traditions, is actually not some individual savior figure. Rather, **Messiah is the idea that the self-reflective human mind, which emerged from the Third Big Bang, has the possibility of jumping to a higher level of consciousness.**

This notion exists in all the great traditions: We will come to a point of complexification and development, beyond which there are two possibilities: Armageddon, in the language of the great traditions—or as we would now say, existential risk—or Messiah, where we jump to a higher level of evolutionary consciousness.

Homo amor is intrinsic to the very fabric of the realization of Cosmos. In systems theory we call this a "minor fluctuation point," when the system is far from equilibrium during a crisis, and jumps the entire system to the next level of order. We are the minor fluctuation point, that da Vinci moment, together with our friends around the world. There are different people playing different parts of the story, but we're at the center of telling this new story together, aiming to be that minor fluctuation point and to jump the entire system to a higher level of order.

In Genesis 29, Leah looks at Judah and for the first time she doesn't see her husband, Jacob—she doesn't use her child to cover over her own emptiness, or to support her marrying "Jacob in the darkness." She's able to move through her trauma and transform. **There's an old saying in Zen Buddhism: "trust people to be who they are." There's a great deal of truth in that—but people can also transform, grow, be more than who you think they are.**

After all, the human being is an expression of the Possibility of Possibility.

Transformation is real, and Leah stands for the possibility of transformation, transforming the traumatic pattern of her life. With her fourth child, Judah, this time she says, "Thank you." And then she hears the Universe say, "You're welcome."

ANTHRO-ONTOLOGY: ACCESSING OUR CLARIFIED DESIRES THROUGH OUR INTERIOR EXPERIENCE

In the *Homo amor* story, Welcome and Mother come together. Judah means thank you, and he becomes the first *Homo amor in the eyes of love*, because he's loved for himself. **He's held by his mother, who loves him madly, as himself, as Judah. He's not instrumental in someone else's game.** Why is Leah able to embrace herself? Why do Leah and Judah, together, become the first *Homo amor*? Because when Leah looks at Judah, and she experiences this radical, wild love for him, she finally understands that she participates in the field of Cosmos. We call that "Anthro-Ontology," which comes from combining *anthro*—human being—with *ontology*, meaning that which is real.

I know that which is Real because it lives in me.

If I deeply clarify my interior, it becomes a source of real knowing, real gnosis, from my own deepest interior experience, my own deepest desires. This is possible because *my interior experience eavesdrops on Divinity*. An ancient text about Noah, the builder of the ark, says, "and God spoke to his heart." The masters say: Noah hears what's going on in the murmurings of the divine heart because Noah has clarified his own heart, so it participates in and expresses the divine heart—one love, one heart. And when Leah looks at Judah in her arms, she feels the welcome she's embracing Judah with, *and she knows that that the Cosmic Welcome is also embracing her.*

Isn't that gorgeous? **She knows that in that experience of welcoming Judah, she's experiencing the welcome that's living in the Cosmos through her.**

We sophisticated Westerners have lost our relationship to the personal face of Cosmos that holds us. We terribly, mistakenly associate that with religious fundamentalism. Culturally, we've forgotten the beautiful tantric principle of non-rejection. Remember: the God you don't believe in doesn't exist, and the prayer that seems ridiculous to you isn't real prayer. Just like we don't associate sexuality with the most degraded forms of pornography, we shouldn't associate the experience of being welcome with the fundamentalist religions that hijacked it, which say that:

- You're only welcome if you fulfill exactly what God told you to do.
- God is quite concerned about what you do when you're naked.
- Make sure not to do too many things that are wrong.

- God only welcomes *my* particular people and not others.
- God welcomes only the good parts of me, not all of me—and certainly not my body or my traumas.

These were the great corruptions in the welcome signs of Cosmos of classical religion. God welcomes only those parts of me that seem holy—and only if I was born to particular people? No! We reject that notion of the personal that's been hijacked, just like degraded forms of pornography hijack sexuality. **We've got to release the hijacker's grip on the interior face of Cosmos, which is infinitely personal.**

Ken Wilber and I articulated the notion that there's "the second face of God," the face of God or Spirit or love that's personal, the Divine that knows my name, that welcomes me. Here's a story that expresses this personal Divine gnosis:

> *There's an oratory competition which features a big prize, based on the best reading of the Psalms, which were written by David, the descendant of Judah. The greatest Shakespearean actor of his time enters and is widely expected to win—no one can really come close. So this actor is reading Psalm 23 in this big Hall in London: "The Lord is my Shepherd; I shall not want. Yea, though I walk through the valley of the shadow of death…" He does this dramatic "Lord is my Shepherd" reading, and he knows how to expertly pitch and modulate his deep, rich voice.*

> *The crowd is absolutely wowed, and when he's done they burst out into wild, enthusiastic applause. They're about to award him the first prize, when this frail old man walks in from the back, all hunched over. He's not invited and he's not on the roster, but he makes his way to the podium; there's this sense that they can't quite stop him, so they graciously let him perform. The old man begins to speak so, so quietly: "The Lord is my Shepherd…"*

He reads slowly, with no elocution, no fancy voice, but as he goes on the place gets quieter and quieter and quieter... until a Silence of Presence fills the room.

He finishes and no one can move. No one can talk. The crowd is stunned, and no one can say anything—until finally one person and then another and the entire place rises and joins in this thunderous ovation that goes on for ten full minutes. No one can stop. The younger Shakespearean actor is a good man, with great skill, but he's obviously missed something. Afterwards, he approaches the old man and says, "I know all the acting techniques, I've trained my whole life, I've played Hamlet and Macbeth and Lear. I know it all. What do you know that I don't?"

And the old man says, "I know the Shepherd."

That's not mere blind faith. In the face of the old man's kind of knowing, this weak faith is ridiculous, trusting something there's no evidence for, that you can't experience in your body, or in your heart and mind. It's mere dogma, completely blind. True faith is about embodied trust—and this kind of trust is *everything*.

I trust the Shepherd.

I trust the Cosmos.

I trust evolution that never forgets a breakthrough.

Forget about the dogma, but do have that experience of *Homo amor*. I'm welcome. Reality is always holding me. **The Mother is always holding me, and because the Mother's holding me, I can be activated, and I can hold Reality.**

Remember, it's always perfect, this sense that I'm at home in Cosmos. You can get there through the world of physics, through molecular biology, through Goodness, Truth and Beauty, through clarified desire and clarified pleasure. And you can get there through uniqueness.

179

HOMO AMOR IS EVOLUTIONARY UNIQUE SELF

Your experience of being unique is not the experience of being generically welcome. We're part of the field of consciousness. That's necessary. That's the first step. I'm not just a separate self. We need to move beyond the experience of separate self and into True Self, but True self is not just being one with the field of consciousness. That's only the beginning of True Self. **There's not only the homogenous field of consciousness; there's also unification with desire and allurement.**

When superficial readers of the original Pali Canon tried to remove desire, they misunderstood, and desire now has a bad name in Buddhism. The field we access in the manifest world is not just a field of pure awareness or consciousness, but also a field of desire. Clarified allurement creates intimate, coherent interconnections between *all* parts in the field.

In CosmoErotic Humanism, we have tried to be both more precise, poetic, and poignant in our description of True Self, which is not only about being "one with" but also about participation. The personal does not disappear. **True Self is the realization that my identity or essence participates directly in the field of consciousness.** So True Self is not evolution beyond ego. It is evolution beyond exclusive identification with ego.

True Self is the realization that my most true identity—my *true* self—participates directly in the field of consciousness, the singular that has no plural. That is a direct felt realization that has been called enlightenment. But even in this state of enlightenment I am also a unique person. My separate self continues to be real in the mind of enlightenment, in the mind of God.

So, consciousness is teaming with Eros, desire, and allurement—it is the direct, participatory experience of the interconnectivity of the All with the All. I feel the field of allurement moving through me. I feel the intimate coherence of all people and all things moving in a perfect dance, animated by the potent precision and poignancy of allurement, Eros, and desire. We all directly participate in the Intimate Universe.

In classical True Self teachings as they are usually expressed, True Self is the direct experience of "I Am." This is indeed true, but partial. True Self is not only I Am, but also allurement and Eros—the pulsing, throbbing character of consciousness itself. True Self participates directly in the spaciousness of Being. But it participates no less in the ecstatic urgency of becoming, coursing through our very essence.

REALITY IS INTIMATE AND RELATIONAL

Nothing is real by itself. There's something real about atoms, but there wouldn't be a single atom whatsoever without the electromagnetic field— no atom can live by itself. In a very real sense, there is no atom—an atom is but a set of allurements, a set of relationships.

Reality is not made of things, but relationships—this is a fundamental category of Reality, all the way up and all the way down. There's no atom without the Higgs field, or the nebula that birthed the star, or the supernova that ended it to create the atom. We call the atom a "thing," and yet we don't include in the atom any of these dimensions of its identity. Should we make the atom non-intimate? We have this image of a world made of these discrete particles called atoms—this is not true. I can study the biology of a plant, but in doing so I can deaden myself to the real plant. I can know its name, its Latin name, its genetics, and its genus, its species, and its medicinal properties, its chemical properties—but I want to feel the plant, in its web of relationships, and let it enter me to know that it doesn't live individually.

This plant is part of an entire web of relationships, without which there is literally no plant. Like everything in the Cosmos, the plant is a set of relationships, governed by allurement and intimacy, which (we may recall) is the set of shared identities in the context of relative otherness, relationships that also involve:

- Mutualities of recognition
- Mutualities of pathos

- ◆ Mutualities of value
- ◆ Mutualities of purpose

As far as we're even able to describe the indescribable Tao, this is the true, intimate nature of Reality. The realization of True Self, at its core, is the realization that nothing exists independently of anything else. Once I know that, I experience myself as a unique node, a unique crystallization of the entire allured intimate system. I'm an irreducibly unique expression of the whole, and as such I know that I'm:

- ◆ Recognized by the whole.
- ◆ Intended by the whole.
- ◆ Desired by the whole.
- ◆ Adored by the whole.
- ◆ Chosen by the whole.
- ◆ Needed by the whole.

Then I can begin to feel at home in True Self as I rest in the field of consciousness. I feel even more at home when I deepen the realization of True Self to include the intimate, interconnected coherence of the All with the All, in the true realization that *Reality is relationships*. In the example we mentioned before, I'm welcome *because* I'm recognized as Unique Self, sitting at that table where I was "welcomed" but didn't quite feel at home—when all of a sudden the hosts desperately need me, my gifts, and my unique quality of being. In that moment I know am welcome.

This, in fact, is always the consciousness of the realized Unique Self. I am always desperately needed. But desperation is often subtle, even hidden.

For example, I walk into a restaurant and there's a waitress supporting two children at home. She was up all night taking care of one of them who was sick. She feels tired and unrecognized and alone and she approaches my table. I naturally say, "Hi, I'm Marc—what is your name?" And without saying anything else those words are invested with a quiet dignity and respect she will literally feel, perhaps not even realizing the source.

Something will shift inside, and her entire day may change direction. I know this is true. I have experienced it.

Similarly, whenever someone says, "Thank you," and we respond, "You're welcome," we pour all of our energy, all of our Outrageous Love and Eros into that "you're welcome"—and in so doing **we begin to activate Reality**.

Most religious people have historically claimed that they're the chosen people; they have hijacked the Messianic impulse. We've got to evolve out of this tendency, moving from egocentric intimacy to ethnocentric intimacy. We've got to welcome the body, our wounds, our own evolutionary transformation, our sexuality, the fullness of our Eros, our brokenness, the holy and the broken Hallelujah, the emergence of the feminine, universal human rights, and the scientific method. Once we've fully and truly welcomed all of that, the nascent Fourth Big Bang—Judah, *Homo amor*, Evolutionary Unique Self—can truly and finally emerge. And because *Homo amor* is welcome, *Homo amor* can turn back to the world itself and say, *Welcome*. That's the beginning of the new story of CosmoErotic Humanism.

BECOMING *HOMO AMOR*: TRANSFORMING UNIQUE SHADOW INTO UNIQUE SELF

I can't become *Homo amor* without a Leah breakthrough moment. Leah is not merely a historical figure, but an archetypical energy of humanity ascending and striving and feeling towards *Homo amor*. Leah lives in me, and I live in her. Leah is uniquely wounded. **We're all holy and broken Hallelujahs; we're all uniquely wounded.**

As I felt my own Leah, I felt where I would "marry Jacob in the darkness," which is an expression of my unique wound, or Unique Shadow.

It's only when I transform Unique Shadow into Unique Self, when I transform my wound into my gift, that I become Homo amor.

Pseudo-eros means covering over the Unique Wound, the Unique Shadow. Eros means there's no avoidance, no *a-void-dance*—I never dance around the void—I walk right through it. You can only trust a person who can walk through the void with you, someone who can look at their shadow. **You don't know a person until you've met their shadow. Until you really see them respond to the worst kind of challenge, you don't know who they are.** You don't even know who you're talking to.

When people go out with people, they send their respectable double for most of the first year. They rarely show up as themselves. But you don't know a person until you get to that moment of crisis—and our crisis is our birth, the crisis that births *Homo amor* in us. Crisis is our evolutionary drive, the unique emergency that generates a unique emergence.

CONTEMPLATION EXERCISE: THE GIFT IS IN THE SHADOW—WHAT'S MY LEAH MOMENT?

The gift is in the shadow, the light that comes from the darkness. I become Homo amor only by moving through my Leah moment.

What kind of major or minor crises have you passed through in your life? What elements of unique shadow appeared? Were they, in retrospect, moments of birthing something new? Journal about this for fifteen to twenty minutes.

4.4

WHEN WE DON'T HAVE SHARED VALUES, WE POLARIZE INTO CERTAINTY

A long-time teacher and friend shared with me a few years ago that when she first came to teach at the prestigious academy where she worked, everyone assumed that there was something called the Good, the True, and the Beautiful. Even though they didn't quite know what it was, it was still a given. All the students took it for granted, and all the teachers took it for granted. Forty years later, none of the teachers assume that there's any intrinsic value of the Good, the True, and the Beautiful—and neither do any of the students. During the time these teachers were active, a former student at this academy named Mark Zuckerberg created Facebook. These things are not unrelated.

There's generally considered to be no shared ground of value, largely because of the ascendancy of several recent, interconnected trends.

First, there's the deconstruction of value based on the postmodern narrative that dominates culture at the moment, spread most prominently through academia and the media.

Second, the computer, which is the physical infrastructure, the exteriorization of the postmodern mind, expresses its interior values, which claims there *is* no narrative of value. **You no longer have to read deeply, merge with a book, track the author, and understand the plotline. There is no plotline to Reality when you superficially jump from website to website.** Your short-term memory, according to the best studies, doesn't even become long-term memory because the digital world is designed to interrupt your attention. In sum:

Postmodernity has deconstructed value—and the computer has deconstructed narrative.

4.5

PREMODERN, MODERN AND POSTMODERN CERTAINTY

When we're desperate for an enemy, and we don't have a sense of intrinsic shared value, we polarize into certainty—lots of people have certainties that they have no grounds for holding. This polarization is one of the key contributing factors to existential risk.

These certainties are quite different from the Judah certainties. The certainties of the premodern era create tribalization and local competition. Every tribe—whether a state or an empire like the Holy Roman or the Ottoman Empire—is animated by a religion that says: we have the truth, and you don't. The enemy of certainty in the premodern era is doubt, which is identified with the devil.

Modernity, however, looks at all interior certainties with suspicion and throws them out—David Hume asserted that, metaphysically, they cannot exist. There's a straight line from this to Wittgenstein and logical positivism, emergent from modernity, neo-Darwinism and existentialism, and then into postmodernity—from Humean skepticism to deconstruction. In fact, Habermas pointed out that postmodernity is just "hypermodernity," modernity on steroids, when the seeds that were sown finally bear their fruit: **In modernity, there's no actual, real, intrinsic sense of value**

that can be seen directly—and the only real certainty is thought to be scientific knowledge through empirical experimentation.

In postmodernity, the claim is that nothing *whatsoever* can be certain. Even those things you assumed were certain, the things you based your life on, like science—even those are not certain either.

Religious certainty overreaches—Barack Obama gave a famous interview where he communicated the popular postmodern position, saying, "I think religion at its best comes with a big dose of doubt. I'm suspicious of too much certainty in the pursuit of understanding, because people are limited. I look at all the damage done around the world in the name of religion and certainty." This notion that certainty is dangerous has a lot of truth to it, but it is partial. This can be contrasted with premodern religious sentiment, which asserts that if you're lost in nihilistic uncertainty, you must embrace our certainty, a sense of "it is true," while the postmodern moment embraces uncertainty.

It is certainly time to move on from here.

4.6

GIVING UP OUR IDENTITY FOR A DEEPER CERTAINTY

Judah, or *Homo amor*, does not say that *dogma* is true. It's not *it is true*, but *I Am true*. **If you don't get that I Am true, then you have a collapse of identity.** You discover the truth of your I Am through Eros, which flows through your True Self and your irreducible Unique Self. I Am true, and I am welcome in the Cosmos.

Without the sense of I Am true, I'm liable to be seduced by false certainties, and to generate the pseudo-eros of my own truth. **Without the certainty of I Am true, I generate my identity through false certainties.** This collapse of identity may be avoided for a while by pseudo-erotically creating an outside enemy. As long as we're fighting Russia, for example, we can think that we're in the circle of our identity, because we have our hero's cape on, and it feels good to face the bad guys. When that collapsed, when the Soviet Union all of a sudden disappeared, we didn't have anyone outside the circle to demonize.

Many adhere to the myth promoted by dogmatic scientism that we're all just random molecules, so there couldn't possibly be any ground for essential, inherent value. There's no ground whatsoever for the sense that I Am true, or that I'm a Unique Self. So what do we do? We create false certainties in order to gain a sense of identity. We tribalize and claim all sorts of certainties that we don't have any real confidence in. We haven't factored into our presupposed certainty that in every model, there's a set of unknowns—both known and unknown. The more we work with a model, the more we discover "known unknowns," and then there's arguably many more "unknown unknowns," but of course we can't say for certain.

We cherry-pick our truths, about which we then claim certainty. Scientists certainly often cherry-pick, and the recent "reproducibility crisis," where the findings of key studies were completely unsupported when reproduced, is a key symptom of this lack of integrity. **By cherry-picking our truths, we become sloppy—because we don't have a sense of our own identity, we rush to claim certainties.**

In 2006, a new creation emerged called a Facebook feed, which allows, for example, a liberal who lives across the street from a radical conservative to be able to scroll for days, weeks, or months, and never see the same thing at all. **This communication breakdown exacerbates polarization,** leading to a Reality that never existed before. Social media is an expression of the global intimacy disorder—a non-erotic Universe. Neighbors are now completely alienated from one another because they don't share the same world at all. We're no longer watching the news at night all together. When I grew up in the United States, everybody watched Walter Cronkite. Now, I have absolutely no idea what my neighbor is absorbing. This is contributing to a radical lack of love, a lack of empathy, and ultimately a widespread global intimacy disorder, causing us to cherry-pick our channels, and lock ourselves into silos of false certainty.

My certainty contradicts yours because that's how facts work. Either I'm right, or you're right—and I lose sight of the truth that, in fact, I'm forming my identity through my certainty. Once a person forms their identity through certainty, you can never convince them, because how can you ask a person to give up their identity? There is no possible way to have a conversation, without curiosity or intimacy. There's no vision of a deeper, coherent ground of Goodness, Truth, and Beauty.

Without the core certainty of my irreducible value that lives beyond a political position, what I naturally do is ground my identity in a particular perspective. When that happens, then to give up my perspective I'd have to be willing to give up my identity. But if my sole identity is that position, I will never give it up. Who's going to willingly give up their entire identity?

• • •

In order to demonstrate this, let's take a look at a series of important scenes from *Twelve Angry Men*, depicting the deliberations of a jury after they've heard all the evidence of a murder case of a young man. It seems like the accused is certainly going to jail. Initially, all but one of the jurors feel that he's guilty—based on hunches and speculation and erroneous information, they know *for certain* that he did it.

But then—one by one—they all start to open up, they start to doubt, they start to consider that their assumptions may actually be wrong. Here we get to see how perspective can shift, and the many ways that certainty can be embodied and experienced. It's a beautiful scene, depicting the movement from naive certainty to uncertainty, and then to deeper truth.

MOVIE SCENE: *TWELVE ANGRY MEN*

[A long court case has just wrapped up, and a young man's life now rests with the decision of twelve men. The judge lays out the next steps. The following is an edited transcript of this scene featuring the key moments.]

Judge: You've listened to a long and complex case, about murder in the first degree. Murder is the most serious charge tried in our criminal courts. You've listened to the testimony, you've had the law read to you and interpreted as it applies in this case. It's now your duty to sit down and try and separate the facts from the fancy. One man is dead. Another man's life is at stake. If there's a reasonable doubt in your mind as to the guilt of the accused, then you must bring me a verdict of not guilty. If, however, there's no reasonable doubt, then you must in good conscience find the accused guilty. However you decide, your verdict must be unanimous. In the event that you find the accused guilty, the bench will not entertain a recommendation for mercy. That sentence is mandatory in this case.

[In the deliberation room, the jury immediately gets to work. Juror Eight is the only one willing to vote not guilty, the lone voice of reasonable uncertainty in the room.]

Foreman: Just let's remember we've got a first-degree murder charge here. If we vote guilty, we send the accused to the electric chair. That's mandatory.

Juror Three: Come on, let's vote.

Juror Ten: Yeah. Let's see who's where.

Forman: All right. This has to be a twelve-to-nothing vote either way. That's the law. All those voting guilty raise your hands. Okay... nine... ten... eleven. That's eleven for guilty. Okay, Not guilty.

Foreman: One. Okay, eleven to one, guilty. Now we know where we are.

Juror Ten: Boy-oh-boy. There's always one.

Juror Seven: So what do we do now?

Juror Eight: Well, I guess we talk.

[So they talk, and reasonable doubt is introduced. False certainty starts to unravel a bit.]

Juror Four: It's a very unusual knife. I've never seen one like it. Neither had the storekeeper who sold it to the boy. Aren't you trying to make us accept a pretty incredible coincidence?

Juror Six: I'm just saying a coincidence is possible.

Juror Three: And I'm saying it's not possible.

[Some time has passed, but most still seem convinced that the young man is a murderer, and they are at a stalemate. Juror Eight calls for a secret ballot to see if there is any doubt hiding from view.]

Juror Eight: I have a proposition to make all of you. I want to call for a vote. I'd like you eleven men to vote by secret written ballot. I'll abstain. If there are still eleven votes for guilty, I won't stand alone. We'll take a guilty verdict in to the judge right now. But if anyone votes not guilty, we'll stay and talk this thing out. That's all. If you want to try it, I'm ready.

Juror Three: Well, finally you're behaving like a reasonable man.

Foreman: That sounds fair.

[Ten of the eleven men continue to remain certain and vote guilty, and one has switched to not guilty. So they continue to talk, most of them reluctantly.]

Juror Eight: Let's take two pieces of testimony and try to put them together. First, the old man in the apartment downstairs. He says he heard the boy say, "I'm going to kill you," and a split second later he heard the body hit the floor. One second later. Right?

Juror Two: That's right.

Juror Eight: Second, the woman across the street claimed positively that she looked out of her window and saw the killing through the last two cars of a passing elevated train. Right? The last two cars.

Juror Three: All right, what are you giving us here?

Juror Eight: Now, we agreed that an el train takes about ten seconds to pass a given point. Since the woman saw the stabbing through the last two cars we can assume that the body fell to the floor just as the train passed by. Therefore, the el had been roaring by the old man's window for a full ten seconds before the body hit the floor. The old man, according to his own testimony, hearing "I'm going to kill you" and the body falling a split second later, would have had to have heard the boy make this statement while the el was roaring past his nose. It's not possible that he could have heard it.

[They continue to circle around the truth, and gradually, one after another, the jurors begin to flip. Juror Three has emerged as the voice of retribution, of certainty, and finally Juror Eight confronts him.]

Juror Eight: Ever since we walked into this room you've been behaving like a self-appointed public avenger!

Juror Three: I'm telling you now! Shut up!

Juror Eight: You want to see this boy die because you personally want it, not because of the facts.

Juror Three: Shut up!

Juror Eight: You're a sadist...

Juror Three: I'll kill you.

Juror Eight: You don't really mean you'll kill me, do you?

[Cracks start to appear in Juror Three's argument, as things get heated and personal. More and more jurors switch to not guilty. In the next scene, it appears that Juror Three is about to violently act out against another juror.]

Juror Two: The boy is five feet, seven inches tall. His father was six-two. That's a difference of seven inches. It's a very awkward thing to stab down, into the chest of someone who's more than a half a foot taller than you are.

Juror Three: Give me that. No I'll make myself about six or seven inches shorter, okay?

Juror Two: That's about right. Maybe a little more.

Juror Three: Okay. Let it be a little more. *[Juror Three appears like he's about to stab the other Juror.]*

Jurors: Watch out!

[Through many tense and beautiful scenes of deliberation and discussion, more jurors start to dwell in the uncertainty, and come to a deeper truth. It finally comes to a head when Juror Three breaks down emotionally, sharing his personal story—his identity—revealing why he was so keen on convicting the young man. He finally agrees to the not guilty verdict.]

Juror Three: There's a boy twenty-two years old. I'll tell you about him. When he was nine he ran away from a fight. I saw him. I was so ashamed I almost threw up. So I told him right out. I'm gonna make a man outa you or I'm gonna bust you in half trying. Well, I made a man outa him all right. When he was sixteen we had a battle. He hit me in the face! He's big, y'know? I haven't seen him in two years. Rotten kid! You work your heart out... *[he starts sobbing]*

This is a very important and powerful scene, one very much worth watching in full, just to get all the psychological dynamics at play. Someone's life—and we could say, if we extrapolate, the life of humanity at large—is on the line, and a decision needs to be made. The entire issue at stake is one between certainty and uncertainty. Is there a reasonable doubt? Is there ground for uncertainty?

Eleven out of twelve people come in without actually having looked at the information in any real way, forming a sloppy groupthink identity, ignoring an enormous amount of information—when someone's life is on the line, when a boy is about to be put to death for something he didn't do. One person stands against this—Juror Eight, played by Henry Fonda. When he says "not guilty," someone asks, "What do we do now?" His response is beautiful: "I guess we talk."

At that moment, there's no real conversation to be had, because it's all about identity, which became gorgeously, painfully apparent at the very end of the scene, when Juror Three is crying, and you feel the entirety of his life pain and trauma. In a sense, he's Leah naming her child, *I was hated by my husband*. He screams out his pain and is finally forced to say "not guilty." He gives up—something he never would have done without being utterly pushed against the wall.

It's clear how a false certainty that generates the death of a human being is casually entertained by a group of "twelve angry men," who are fundamentally good men—albeit men who are lazy, sloppy, have no sense of identity, or true grounding in a Universal Grammar of Value. And this movie depicts a time before postmodernity. Now we no longer have the Soviet Union, and we've totally deconstructed all ground of value. Now we're watching the rise of the tech plex, realizing that we probably won't have a job in thirty years, or our children won't. Jobs are a large part of our identity, one of the core structures of family and society, and they are going to disappear.

Many will ask: *Who even am I, then?*

4.7

NOT IT IS TRUE, BUT I AM TRUE: HOLDING UNCERTAINTY, AVOIDING FALSE CERTAINTY

Polarizing into false certainties is so easy to do, and in order to get to a higher certainty, we must be willing to entertain epistemological uncertainty. In the movie, Juror Eight (Henry Fonda) says that **only by holding uncertainty can we get to a higher certainty. By holding uncertainty, we can also avoid a false certainty.**

Those two options are both implicit in *Twelve Angry Men*. We're going to get to the higher certainty of "not guilty," which is accurate in this case. But we also have to avoid a false certainty that creates the death of an individual human being, the first shock of existence—as well as the death of all of humanity, the second shock. **We must be willing to bracket the fusing of our identity with our certainty, be willing to hold uncertainty, be willing to avoid false certainty.** We've begun to re-vision certainty from, "It is true" to "I Am true." It's not that there's *nothing* that's true—lots of things are true—but we must avoid dogma.

• • •

Here is a joke to illustrate a common form of "false uncertainty":

197

There's a man who's married to this very beautiful woman. He says to his son: "You know, I'm not sure your mother is being faithful to me." (It's a little complicated, talking to your kid about all this.) And the son says, "Why are you talking to me about this?" The Father says, "Well, my son, I need your help. I have to find out what's really going on here."

The son doesn't want anything to do with this, but there is that commandment: Honor your father and your mother. You can't deny your father. So he reluctantly agrees. The father says, "Good, I'm going to go out of town this weekend. You watch your mother very carefully, and when I get back you'll tell me what happened."

The father leaves and when he comes back he's dying to talk to his son. When they're finally alone together, he asks, "So what happened?" The son says, "Tata, I'm so sorry, I feel terrible telling you this, but after you left, there was this knock at the door about an hour later, and this big strong, handsome, Russian man shows up. It's clear they recognize each other, and mom gives him a big hug."

The father says, "Okay... but what happened next?"

"Well, she brought him inside and she sat him not just anywhere, but in your chair."

"Okay, and what happened next?"

"Tata, I'm sorry to tell you this, but she went and she brought out your special herring & sponge cake that's only for you, and she gave it to him."

"Oh, this is worse than I thought. What happened next?"

"Well, after that, you know, they went into the bedroom and they shut the door."

"Oh my god, this is terrible... tell me what happened next."

"Tata, you told me I had to, so I had no choice. I looked through the keyhole and I saw them near the bed taking their clothes off."

"This is really bad. What happened next?"

"Well, Tata, I can't tell you—they turned the lights off, so I don't know..."

And the father says: "What? Oh no! The doubt is going to kill me!"

This joke represents "false uncertainty"—where I claim to be uncertain about something when I'm not actually uncertain at all. I know that I'm betrayed. I claim to hold all these different dimensions, but in my body, I actually know what I'm doing, whatever that betrayal means, whether it's a betrayal of another person, or a betrayal of Goodness, Truth, and Beauty.

As an example, Michael Murphy funded very careful empirical, cross-cultural research—what William James would call "radical empiricism"—on 2,500 cases of reincarnation, focusing on reports of children who die and then a short time later, someone in a completely different part of the world is born. Through a solid process of validation, they check to see if there's any connection between the two people at all. Then they check to see if the new kid who's born has, for example, a wound or a mark at the exact place where the first child was killed. They often remember the earlier child's entire life, or many key aspects, and it's verified by an enormous amount of empirical data.

Later in his life, Michael wrote a book called *The Life of the Body,* in which he says, and I'm paraphrasing here: "I got to say that I feel sleazy about this, because for many, many years, people have been asking me what I think about reincarnation. I live in San Francisco, and I want to be kind of politically correct, so until just very recently"—and at this time he was 85 years old—"I would tell people that I'm an agnostic about it, I'm not sure. Actually, I was lying. I have all the information. I've researched this better than most people in the world. I'm absolutely certain that reincarnation is one of the structures of Cosmos; life's not over when it's over as we know it, and the amount of empirical information that verifies it is overwhelming. When people would ask me until recently, I didn't have the courage to say that I'm clear about this. So I said, I was uncertain." That's another example of false uncertainty—where your public expression is at odds with what you know to be true.

Without understanding and being able to hold our uncertainty and certainty, we are left only with win/lose metrics. We have to be willing to hold uncertainty to get to a higher certainty. We have to be willing to let go of our false certainties.

CONTEMPLATION EXERCISE: LISTING YOUR CERTAINTIES

The exercise is simple: list your certainties. What do you know for certain to be true or real or right? Make an actual list of your certainties and claim them. It's a big deal.

Your certainties are welcome home signs from Cosmos.

What are things that you know, that you believe in, that live in you?

Sense into value, goodness, truth, beauty, and claim your own certainties, whatever they are, without judgement. It's critically important to be able to list your certainties.

4.8

FALSE CERTAINTY, ANTHRO-ONTOLOGY, AND UNCERTAINTY AS AVOIDANCE

We're used to talking about how false certainties are dangerous. Obama equated religion with certainty, and viewed them both as damaging, because that's the natural movement of the postmodern mind—and it's not entirely wrong, of course. As Voltaire said, speaking about premodernity: "Remember the cruelties." Clearly, there were lots of false certainties in place in the traditional era that were enormously damaging, just as there were in the modern period. **We need to hold uncertainty to avoid false certainties—not just the false certainties of the premodern traditions, but also the false certainties of our modernist legacy institutions, and current postmodern cultural narratives.**

The false certainties in science lead to scientists not disclosing conflicts of interest, cherry-picking data, or being led by unconscious dogma. Just like we need to distinguish between the best of religion, its depth structures, and the surface shadows of religion and religious fundamentalism, we need to identify interior wisdom practices that follow a rigorous version of the scientific method, based in empirical knowledge resulting from experiments validated by the "community of the adequate." In interior

201

science—i.e., religion—the real depth structures come from practice, from actions followed by results, leading to knowledge.

Let's say I meditate carefully, and experiment carefully, and it generates gnosis of True Self and the irreducible value of uniqueness—*I can actually know things by going inside.* When I go inside, I access true "anthro-ontological" knowledge. Cross-comparing results around the world with people doing different versions of these experiments, we then take the shared universal results, and get to truths of the interior sciences. **In other words, we need to distinguish between the great truths of interior science based in Anthro-Ontology, and the false certainties of many surface structures of religion.**

In the same way, we've got to distinguish between the false certainties of scientism and the valid experimentation of true science. There's an enormous amount of information that's been disclosed over the last ten to twenty years in many academic mainstream articles, which clearly show that science is funded by a set of interested institutions, that it cherry-picks the trials it wants to do, organizes the data it wants to organize, and that the notion "the scientist is always right"—just like "my doctor is always right," "I just listen to my lawyer," and "the teacher is always right"—is not in any way true. These need to be held and seen, just like we hold the false certainties of religion.

• • •

We must also hold our false uncertainties, where we claim to be uncertain about things when there's an enormous amount of information. **Sometimes in our own lives, we use uncertainty as our strategy to avoid commitment.** I avoid a decision through uncertainty, but that's actually a commitment. Inaction *is* a decision. Stepping away is a choice.

> *The failure to make a commitment is also a commitment—to inaction.*

Freud said that we're all geniuses when it comes to self-deception. By claiming and holding uncertainty beyond what I need to, I'm using it to support egoic ends because I'm using it to shape my identity. We hold many distressing disguises of uncertainties which, as Michael Murphy pointed out, are false uncertainties.

Remember the punchline from the joke about the father and son: "The doubt will kill me." We often can't actually bear to look at the truth. And in the case of the joke, I'm not even sure how that truth would transform him—the truth would just hurt him and devastate him. **Often, however, the truth transforms us and sets us free—but we're afraid of that freedom.** We're too afraid of giving up our old pseudo-identities and pseudo-erotic tendencies to fully step in. We keep repeating and doing the same things again and again.

As such, *Homo amor* must be in a dialectical dance between certainty and uncertainty.

4.9

FALSE CERTAINTY AND OBSCENE RELIGIOUS EXPLANATIONS OF SUFFERING

In this moment of hyper-polarization, we need to *transcend* polarization and create a new shared ground of understanding. A number of years ago, Deepak Chopra gave a lecture at Caltech, and a physicist named Leonard Mlodinow challenged him on his physics. Deepak later made an offer: "Let's get together and talk about religion. We'll study Spirit, and we'll study physics." And they did—they got together and wrote a book called *The War of the Worldviews*, which, of course, is all about polarization.

It's an interesting read. Both Chopra and Mlodinow keep marshalling their facts, and both of them are cherry-picking information—on the physics side, and on the Spirit side. There's polarization, but there's always something going on underneath it. **Often, the reason why a person holds their position has to do with a core value they're holding, or a core value that they feel will be violated if they hold a different position.**

At one point in the book, Mlodinow is telling the story of his mother. He represents the scientific view, which is rapidly evolving, but often unconsciously assumes the materialist view that the universe is empty, random, and has no inherent meaning. Deepak counters that this is a heartless view of life. Mlodinow responds, and I'm paraphrasing here: "My mother, now almost ninety years old, told me once of a cold day when she was about seventeen and the war was raging in Europe. Her town in Poland was occupied by the Nazis.

Now, on this day, one of those Nazis told a few dozen of the town's Jews, including my mother, to line up in a row and kneel in the snow. He walked along the row and every few steps, leaned down, put his gun into someone's head and fired. The spiritual view says that my mother's survival was not random."

His mother wasn't shot, so—in the spiritual view—does this not imply that there was a cosmic reason for those who were slaughtered?

Most of the members of my parents' families were killed during the Holocaust. To me, this spiritual explanation also feels cold and heartless. Who can say why they were not saved? That's what Mlodinow is holding. That's what's driving him. He's claiming that religion tries to give explanations for suffering, and he's saying, "I'm not buying it."

And I'm with him. I'm not buying it either.

Spirituality that deadens our sensitivity to pain and evil and suffering, and tries to easily explain away evils with what are called "theodicies," is not acceptable.

Mlodinow sets up a kind of heartless spirituality against his preferred option, which says, "I am not willing to be so heartless." This happens often: A caricature of a view is set up, sparking a "war of worldviews." I came to the same conclusion about bad readings of religion that Mlodinow did. **Because just as there's bad science, there's also bad religion.**

I remember when I was young and I read a book by a guy named Hanoch Teller, who tells the story about this man who always did good deeds for people. One time, on the way to the airport, he was doing something to help his cab driver, which caused him to miss his plane. He was supposed to get home for his daughter's birthday party, and was afraid to call his wife because he knew she'd be furious. He waited until the plane was supposed to have touched down and calls his wife. She screams with joy when he calls, because the plane had crashed.

Teller's point is that because this man had done all these good deeds, he had been saved. But what about all the other people who died in the crash? Did their lack of good deeds result in their deaths? At that moment, I broke with my tradition a bit, and spent a year of my life reading day and night. I wrote a set of two books in Hebrew, challenging this wrong reading in religion and finding the deeper sources.

One book is called *Vadai*, which means *Certainty*, and the other is called *Safek*, which means *Uncertainty*.[11] I took Mlodinow's position, because a spirituality that creates explanations for suffering, justifications for suffering—he was saved because he was doing good deeds, or others weren't because they did bad things—is utterly obscene. I wrote *Certainty* and *Uncertainty* because those two don't oppose each other.

We've got to be able to hold the certainty and the uncertainty together.

I hold the certainty that *I Am true*. I receive all of the welcome home signs in Cosmos that we've articulated—Goodness, Truth, Beauty, Value, the gorgeous and coherent intimacies of science, the Eros of the Cosmos, all the way down and up, the unexpected brilliance of mathematics, etc.—all of it.

---

[11] *Certainty (VADAI): From It Is True to I Am True* and *Uncertainty (SAFEK): Reclaiming Uncertainty as a Spiritual Value.*

If I ask anyone whether it's all meaningful or none of it is meaningful at all—I find that no one will assert that nothing's meaningful, because we actually experience, every day, in our lives, that our choices do matter. **We experience a sense that it matters how I talk to the person next to me, that there are better and worse choices.** Howard Bloom and I have written an essay that traces the development of meaning, exploring how in fact meaningful choices are made in the world of matter.

Contrary to popular belief, atoms and molecules have some degree of choice. Freeman Dyson also discusses the notion of an elemental proto-freedom—not the kind of freedom humans have, of course, but a kind of proto-freedom that lives very early on, that goes deep down, all the way down. Stuart Kaufman, the great complexity theorist and mathematician, also points to this proto-freedom that exists in Reality, as does Whitehead.

All of our certainties do not cancel out our holy uncertainty.

In other words, **past religious traditions often made a great mistake in wanting to make everything certain.** And what's more uncertain than our understanding of why there's evil in the world? I'm not going to try and extend my certainty, I'm not going to overreach my certainty, I'm not going to explain to you why Leonard Mlodinow's mother experienced those horrors, or why my mother saw a two-year-old baby ripped apart in front of her eyes.

No, we're not going to explain them away. It's a mystery. We. Have. No. Fucking. Idea.

It wasn't to make anyone a better person. It wasn't karmic retribution; we reject all the attempts of theodicy to give any sort of "explanation." *We hold the radical uncertainty of it.* **We refuse to deface the mystery with false certainty. We don't let our certainties cancel our uncertainty—but we also don't let the uncertainty cancel our certainty.**

207

ALL POLARIZATION HAPPENS WHEN YOU ARE OUTSIDE THE FIELD OF VALUE

Our certainties are real. How do we live with them, together with our uncertainties? All polarization happens when we're outside the Tao, outside the field of consciousness and value—when we're *not actually in the Eros of Reality*. **But in fact, we can never really be out of the field. No matter where we think we are, we're always in the Field of Value.** You're always in the field of consciousness. Always held.

We're always already in the Tao.

We can only *think* we're out of it. We're asleep to the Tao, not experiencing that which is omnipresent—when I'm asleep, I haven't actually opened up to the Field of She, the Goddess, and I've stepped out of Eros. The Eye of the Heart opens up the Field of the Tao, and our perception is expanded. In Aramaic, it's called the "Field of Holy Apples."

The *Tao Te Ching* said it very beautifully: "The knowledge which is knowable is not the eternal knowledge. The Tao that is speakable is not the eternal Tao. Naming gives rise to the 10,000 things." The 10,000 things of this world can obscure you from the Tao. The Tao is non-conceptual gnosis, an intrinsic knowing about the nature of what is, that lives in me, that I can *taste*. Aquinas' favorite verse in the David-Judah lineage, from Psalms, is: "Taste and see that the Lord is good."

We're deeply aware of suffering. We don't create false certainties. **We hold the uncertainty, but when we're in the Tao, we're in Eros,** *and we can hold the contradiction, which gives way and becomes paradox.*

We never live in paradise—*the only paradise is paradox.*

Outside of the Tao, there's no Eros, only pseudo-eros, words, conceptual structures. Pseudo-erotic structures contradict other pseudo-erotic structures. They can't be held together because we're outside of the circle, outside the wider Field of Value. We often think: either I believe in individual autonomy, or I believe in communion, in the community. It's either separate self or social self.

Autonomy and communion, when they're outside the Tao, outside the field of consciousness, outside of True Self/Unique Self—they contradict each other.

But you can absolutely have the experience of being completely with someone, or completely connected to the group, *and* being completely free and autonomous. *The contradiction between autonomy and communion dissolves in ecstasy,* **which is a quality of the Tao.** Aristotle's Law of Excluded Middle, which says that two contradictory terms cannot both be true, only works outside the Tao.

4.10

HOLDING PARADOX WITH LAUGHTER, AND EXPRESSING OUTRAGEOUS LOVE IN RESPONSE TO INJUSTICE

In order to further explore paradox and the dangers of false certainty, let me share another joke:

> So this guy dies, and he's very religious, very righteous. He's so righteous that they're willing to give him an exclusive audience with God. The angels are pretty excited—he has a meeting with God, and because he's so righteous, he gets to do whatever he wants to do. He can sing a song, he can chat, he can ask for knowledge, he can ask for power, whatever he wants to do. The angels usher him into the divine chamber and they say, "Okay, you got it, the floor is yours. Ask anything, say anything." You'd expect him to ask for wisdom or power or whatever it is, but instead he says, "Well, I actually just want to tell God a joke." The angels respond, "You want to tell God a joke? Are you for real? Okay, well, it's your floor. Do whatever you want." So he tells God a joke—a Holocaust joke.

When he's done, God kinda looks at him and says, "I don't get it."

Then the guy says: "Hmmmm, well I guess you had to be there."

In this joke about the Holocaust—about my mother's Holocaust, about Leonard Mlodinow's Holocaust, the Armenian Holocaust, the Holocaust in Rwanda—the righteous man goes to heaven and gets to talk directly to God, but decides to tell a joke.

Why is he telling a joke? *Because only laughter can hold paradox.*

There's a small text from 2,200 years ago called *The Book of Creation* that lists twelve—not just five—faculties of perception. Laughter is definitely a faculty of perception that tells me things about Reality that no other faculty of perception can tell me.

I taste—I know one thing.

I smell—I know something else.

I feel—I know something else.

I see—I know something else.

I hear—I know something else.

Each faculty of perception accesses a different terrain or texture of the interior and exterior of Reality. **What does laughter do? It nullifies the illusion.** That's why jokes bring down tyrannies and dictatorships—and laughter allows us to hold paradox. The man in this joke goes to talk to God, meaning he's in the story—*he's in the Tao.* This is his reward for being righteous. He tells God a Holocaust joke. When God says, "I don't get it," He says, "I guess you had to be there"—in other words: *Where the fuck were You?!*

You begin to see the paradox here. People who polarize, those with only one paltry perspective, lose a sense of irony and a sense of paradox. They disqualify all other values, while desperately holding on to their identities.

211

CHALLENGING GOD IN RIGHTEOUS ANGER

Here's another example of the need to hold multiple perspectives in paradox. In Elie Wiesel's first book, *Night*, which won the Nobel Prize in 1986, there's a boy hanging on the gallows in Auschwitz, and Wiesel says, "Where's God? God's hanging on the gallows"—meaning God is challenged, put on trial, and found guilty. But then, a few years later, he writes a series of books about Judah and Leah and Abraham and Moses and Jeremiah. Then he writes a book called *Souls on Fire* about the great mystics, masters of the interior sciences. These books hold deep reverence for the Divine. **These perspectives are both utterly necessary, and we need to find a way to somehow hold both the reverence for and the challenge to the divine. To move into *Homo amor*, we must be able to hold multiple perspectives.**

When I'm in the *Tao*, I've moved from pseudo-eros to Eros.

I'm *Homo amor*, not Homo armor.

I'm a unique expression of the field.

I'm both Judah, and I'm Leah.

Now I can hold paradox.

I can hold certainty. I can hold uncertainty. **And I can hold them both, *together*.**

And to do this, we've got to become Outrageous Lovers. Outrage means that first we have to get angry. We have to put God on trial. We are *furious*. It's unbelievable.

• • •

There's this incredible story about Judah's great grandfather, Abraham. He's having this mystical conversation with God, and God says, some people did some bad shit. Sodom and Gomorrah, these guys are bad people. They got to be destroyed. That's the Divine decree. They've committed every manner of moral evil—the worst kinds—so they have to be killed.

212

So Abraham says: "You can't do that."

God says: "Hello? I'm God, remember: omniscient, omnipotent…"

And Abraham says something like, "Well, I'm *Homo amor* and I'm omni-considerate for the sake of the whole…"

I remember being twenty-six years old and reading a book by one of the most popular lecturers today in the religious world named Akiva Tatz. He's a good man, but he says that the spiritual person must be all about certainty, and they do not entertain uncertainty. He tries to prove this by saying the word *safek*, "uncertainty," doesn't appear anywhere in the Bible.

However, *safek* is a post-Biblical word—the older Hebrew word for uncertainty is *ullai*, which means "maybe." And there's at least six "maybe" stories in the book of Genesis alone—all of them pivoting around *ullai*, uncertainty. Judah is the certainty moment, but there are six key "maybe" stories.

One of them is this one, about an outraged Abraham who challenges the Divine when God is about to destroy the corrupt cities of Sodom and Gomorrah. Abraham protests: "You can't do this—maybe there are fifty righteous people in the city." God says, "No way, man." "Well, maybe there's forty?" God says, "No, it's not happening." "Maybe there's thirty, maybe there's twenty, maybe there's ten?" God: "It's settled." Abraham says, "I don't give a flying fuck about the facts, you can't do this! You can't just destroy the city."

Abraham turns to the Divine and he says, *will the Judge of the whole world not do justice?*

He gets angry.

Levi Isaac of Berdichev, who lived in the nineteenth century, was madly in love with the Divine, and saw welcome signs everywhere. He lived in True Self exponentialized, everywhere. This was one of the major figures in Elie Wiesel's book *Souls on Fire*. One of things Levi Isaac did, in the face of so much outrageous suffering, was to put God on trial. He called to the witness stand orphans, widows, people who fall asleep alone, crying desperately for someone else in their bed, all those who have been betrayed, many others… At the end of the trial, after God fails to speak in his defense, Levi Issac finds him guilty on all counts.

He finally says: "God, I find you guilty, but I love you anyways for all you've done."

After finding God totally guilty, he goes and prays to God. That's Outrageous Love.

My good friend John was the chair of the Center for a long time. He said, "Marc, you gotta stop this Outrageous Love thing. Let's call it 'unlimited love' instead." No, it's outrageous, because *rage* is there, right at the heart of it, animating it. It's called the rage of the prophet. We've got to hold together radical love *and* radical anger. The Hebrew word, *hema*, commonly translated as "anger," actually means love and anger at the same time.

So it's Outrageous Love. **Rage is absolutely vital—and I have to own it before I move through it. We can't avoid it.**

What does it mean to get angry? Think of that famous scene from the movie *Network*, where a famous anchor Howard Beale (played by Peter Finch) goes on live TV with an impassioned rant that captures the zeitgeist so perfectly—all about crime and the economy of 1970s America. He coins the popular catch-phrase, "I'm mad as hell, and I'm not going to take it anymore!" He then encourages everyone across the nation to shout it from their windows. It's a powerful scene, a vital expression of righteous anger.

I'm mad as hell, and I'm not going to take it anymore—I'm a human being and my life has value. That's Outrageous Love. That's the rage in Outrageous Love. That's Levi Isaac of Berdichev, who puts a God he loves on trial. It's not mere human sentiment, which is a strategy of the ego to gain some comfort in the win/lose metrics of life.

It's Outrageous Love, Evolutionary Love. It's the love at the heart of existence itself—and it's outrageous.

Let's add a dimension here because it's going to hold love and rage together. What happens when the postmodern deconstruction of value comes along, and we can no longer have a shared sense even of what this sentence means: *my life has value? Network* was made while the Russians were still in space, when there was still an enemy out there. Modernity was in hyper-mode, and postmodernity hadn't yet broken out as a dominant cultural narrative.

WHERE AND WHY—*AYEH*

Let's step in now more fully. We're in the Tao together. We're in the Field of Value. *Homo amor* is always in the Field of Value.

How do we relate to evil? The Great question arises in response to suffering—*why*? Why is there suffering? When we ask about the question of suffering—when we scream, *it's not fair*—what are we saying? Where is the justice? In fact, in Hebrew where and why are the same word, *ayeh.*

To answer these questions prematurely and claim certainty would be to overreach and deny uncertainty—this would destroy *Homo amor.* If *Homo amor* denies the mystery, then *Homo amor* has died before even beginning. **Homo amor has to embrace the mystery.**

When I embrace the mystery and I'm in the Tao, I move from contradiction to paradox.

And what if I try and answer the question *why?*

In Dostoyevsky's *The Brothers Karamazov*, when Alyosha and Ivan have their great dialogue right after they've watched a group of hounds rip a boy apart, Ivan says, "I don't want anything to do with your God." He means: I don't want anything to do with your theodicy, with your explanations, your justifications. Ivan is completely right here, but he understands and interprets his position wrongly. He understands the world and this contradiction only in a *polarized* way. He's stepped out of the Field of Value:

Where one is able to hold paradox.

Where one is able to dance fluidly between certainty and uncertainty.

Where one is able to laugh.

Where one is also able to scream out—and *must* scream out.

Where one is able to love, outrageously—as *Homo amor*.

So as *Homo amor*, we must call out and ask *why?* and *where?*—and the particular phrase in the liturgy is, **where is God?**

We have to find a way to ask why and where that holds and honors the mystery.

CHAPTER 5

FIRST PRINCIPLES
& FIRST VALUES

5.1

GROUNDING THE NEW STORY
IN REAL VALUE

We'll begin this chapter with a recapitulation of our intention, and recommitting to finding our place in the Intimate Universe—showing up, waking up, and growing up into that Intimate Universe. We are striving to make contact with the Infinity of Intimacy, as it lives in us and as we live in it. We've alluded to many pieces so far, and we now want to bring them all together.

ARCHIMEDES: GIVE ME A LEVER AND FULCRUM AND I'LL MOVE THE WORLD

Imagine that you're building a house, or building a company, or building an entrepreneurial vision, and you see that there's a linchpin, something that can hold it all together. As Archimedes said, "Give me a lever with the right fulcrum and I'll move the world." **We need a lever that allows you to move the whole thing.** There are certain pivotal moves in culture that are invisible, and if you could only move them, then:

- You could bring down tyranny.
- You could evolve the source code of culture and consciousness.
- You could recreate, move, shape, and revision the world.

That's exactly what da Vinci was doing in Florence—looking for levers that could change the world. We've been alluding to such levers all week. In some sense, the Dharma, CosmoErotic Humanism, and the New Story address many of them, but underneath all of them there's **a primary lever**—that's often invisible—without which nothing else moves.

- There's no Outrageous Love.
- There's no Phenomenology of Eros.
- There's no *Homo amor*.
- There's no Role Mate, Soul Mate, and Whole Mate.
- There's no Unique Self Symphony.

None of it moves without this lever: We need to turn towards First Principles and First Values.

It's easy to want to do this very quickly, but let's see if we can take this step by step. Each step is major, and we're obviously not going to do it all in one chapter. We're going to try and see the big picture. We're going to try and see the scaffolding. We're going to try and see the vision. Let's take this stage by stage.

A NEW STORY BASED ON FIRST PRINCIPLES AND FIRST VALUES IS THE ONLY THING THAT CAN ADEQUATELY RESPOND TO EXISTENTIAL RISK

Only a New Story can respond to existential risk. That's our first premise. You can't respond to existential risk without telling a New Story. However—and here's the big however—in Nadav Eyal's great new book *Revolt*, he tries to tell a new story. The last chapter, in fact, is called, "A New Story." The problem is that his new story is about all sorts of (great and necessary) technical, infrastructural, economic, political, social reforms that he suggests throughout the book. But then he asks: how are we going to hold all these things together? He says it would be possible if we had shared values, *but of course we can't have shared values—how could you possibly have shared values*? In our postmodern context, it's not possible to talk about shared values intrinsic to Cosmos because there are no such values like that. He basically says, *We all know that there are no preordained or eternal values.*

Now, Eyal is a sweet guy, but he's a reporter—not a thinker. When he says there are no eternal or preordained values, he's just repeating what he heard in school, like so many. That's what he heard through culture and internalized. We used to have an idea of preordained and eternal values; now we don't anymore, and so Nadav struggles. He doesn't quite understand how we can create a new story because what's going to bind us together? For Nadav, there's nothing you can do about that, because the old idea that there's intrinsic value is obviously just not true—that's a given. **His new story is therefore not at all compelling because it's a technocratic set of solutions in a world that doesn't have a shared discourse, a shared language, a shared set of protocols, a shared culture, or a shared grammar of value.**

Let's just say that only a New Story can respond to existential risk—but in order for a New Story to be real, to be compelling, for it to take hold, it can't be a story that we made up. It can't be mere conjecture.

My dear, wonderful, evolutionary Whole Mate Barbara Marx Hubbard, in these matters of New Story, would always say, "I *declare* the New Story." She did it so elegantly and so well and so beautifully. But then I would say, "Barbara, you can't just declare the New Story." We've got to ground it in Reality. In other words, **the New Story** is **grounded in the sciences, and in all of the various wisdom traditions.** We show that it's implicit everywhere, that this story is fully and absolutely true, and it's grounded in a set of values that are real.

THE INVISIBLE STORY THAT DRIVES EVERYTHING

Showing exactly what the New Story is—and that story operates everywhere—is found in books like *Tenets of Intimacy*, *Outrageous Love*, the *Homo amor* books, and the *Eros* books. In those volumes, we go through the actual principles and show how they operate all the way up and all the way down in Cosmos.

For now, we want to clearly show that a New Story based on First Principles and First Values is the *only thing* that can adequately respond to existential risk. *Why is that the case?*

Recall the two major generator functions—or root causes—of existential risk: the first is a failed story, the current operating system of culture that lives in all of us. This disastrous story plays out in companies, in teachers unions, in families, in schools, everywhere: **rivalrous conflict governed by win/lose metrics**.

Whether you're in a company, a subdivision of a company, a part of the government, in a hospital, in a political party, or a social organization— it doesn't matter. Every organization—whether it's philanthropic, institutional, or corporate—it runs on rivalrous conflict. There's always win/lose metrics and the implicit story is: *I have to be successful.* According to win/ lose metrics, success means that I've been rewarded in a particular way that makes me stand out and that gives me a dimension of status and comfort. If I'm not successful in win/lose metrics, then I'm devalued and feel like my life's missing something essential. We value the structure of success—across the board. **Rivalrous conflict governed by win/lose metrics is transcultural, the reigning story in the world, the source code, the operating system—but here's the key: it's invisible.** You often can't see it.

You think you're living your life with agency and autonomy, but it's very difficult to fight a source code that has invisible playgrounds in your mind. "We all live in inescapable frameworks," wrote Charles Taylor in *Sources of the Self.* Our current inescapable framework—introduced by modernity— is what we're calling Success 2.0: productive achievement in which you're always competing in rivalrous conflict. It replaced Success 1.0 from the premodern, traditional period, which said: "Be obedient to God, and follow the rules."

This new win/lose success story now drives everything.

5.2

COMPLICATED SYSTEMS VERSUS COMPLEX SYSTEMS

You bring that dominant story of culture together with our interrelated socio-economic system, created in Bretton Woods in 1944, near the end of the second World War. We wanted to interconnect the world economically, through trade, currency, and supply chains, so there could never be another world war. It's part of the reason why there hasn't been one since then—only smaller proxy wars in other countries. In that sense, it's been successful, but seventy-five years later, **we've got a vast system of interconnected parts that tragically do not communicate with or see each other**. And these interconnected subsystems are all operating according to win/lose metrics—based, for example, on quarterly reports.

You've got very thin and fragile supply lines, and you've got financial instruments that affect other financial instruments, with cascading effect on other financial instruments all through the world, that don't see each other. **The world's enormously fragile.** For example, recall America's inability to get masks when Covid broke out, as people were dying all over the country because they couldn't get masks. Even doctors and nurses were initially unable to get masks. There were no masks because the nature of global contracts and global supply chains meant that they were all made overseas:

- We don't have local commerce—it's global.
- We don't have local production—it's global.
- We don't have local agriculture systems—they're global.
- We don't have local currencies—they're global.
- We don't have local financial infrastructure—it's global.

The entire system is interrelated and optimized for "success"—which, according to our dominant success story, means *efficiency* and *short-term profit*. This brings us to the second generator function of existential risk: the entire system is "complicated," or what Nassim Taleb called "fragile," rather than a robust, "anti-fragile," or "complex" system.

One way to understand what a fragile, complicated system is, in our understanding, that there's no allurement between the parts. A Ferrari is an example of a complicated system. The parts are put together in a very precise way—**they fit together, but** *are not allured to each other*. This means that if they stop making a part, or if the factory closes down, that's it. The system breaks down easily:

- Any breakdown undermines the system and it doesn't regenerate.
- It doesn't take care of its waste—it creates externalities.
- It doesn't naturally grow or develop.

Conversely, an anti-fragile, complex system means that there is allurement between the parts. For example, a Brazilian rainforest is a vast, complex system, but the system works together:

- There's an ecological harmony and balance.
- The parts communicate with each other.
- There's a relationship between the soil, the insects, the trees, the air, and the animals.
- Waste is created—and fully absorbed into and used and recirculated by the system.
- There are no dead zones.

223

So to recap, the two generator functions for existential risk are:

- A Dangerous Global Success Story: Rivalrous conflict governed by win/lose metrics as the world's main operating system.
- A Complicated Global System: A system that is fragile and prone to massive breakdowns, rather than a complex system that's allured, anti-fragile, harmonious, and self-sustaining.

These generator functions will lead to one or several of the current existential or catastrophic risk scenarios. For example, if we had two or three basic food staples wiped out by climate change for two years in a row, the fragile, non-intimate nature of global supply chains are such that around three billion people would die.

It doesn't need to be this way.

5.3

GLOBAL INTIMACY DISORDER

These two generator functions do not quite get at the core of it yet. They are both important to identify, but ultimately point to something deeper. The name we're giving to the prime generator function of existential risk is: Global Intimacy Disorder. We can see this in complicated systems: *there's no intimacy between the parts*, so there's fragility in the system. The entire financial market collapsed in 2008 because there was no allurement between the parts. We couldn't see each other or feel each other: a global intimacy disorder.

The rivalrous success story based on win/lose metrics means: every time I see you, I don't see You, a Thou, a human being. Instead, I see an "it," an object in my game that I can benefit from. It's *thank you, we've exchanged favors, now I owe you, or you owe me.* There's no true *welcome.*

So how do we heal a global intimacy disorder? What do we need to do? What's the first step?

We restore intimacy.

We all need to get to this place where we understand that the issue is a global intimacy disorder. It sounds easy enough to say, but it took us at least ten years of reading, formulating, re-formulating, discussing, and going through an enormous amount of literature across many disciplines, just to try and get to the root of it. Once you say it, it's like, *oh! of course*—it really is the root cause. **And being able to cut through to the root, to the core diagnosis, is half the solution.**

Nadev Eyal's *Revolt* cannot offer a diagnosis. He has only a vague sense of the deeper issues at play, and he dismisses inherent, intrinsic value because he's caught in the postmodern narrative that denies its very possibility. Value is simply not the subject of his book, nor could it be—from a postmodern cultural frame, it's completely off limits. He tries to figure out what structural changes we can make, which is helpful as far as it goes. But the feeling of the last chapter is pretty hopeless because you really can't do deep and lasting transformation without grounding the New Story in true and real value.

RESTORING INTIMACY

So our diagnosis is a global intimacy disorder, and we know we need to restore intimacy. But how do we do that? Let's say we're dealing with a couple. It could be two friends, two partners, a husband and a wife, some version of a couple.

Here's the deep truth, just between us: most marriage counseling doesn't work because you're usually only dealing with the symptoms—but you've got to go to the root. **And the root is: does the couple have a shared story?**

If you have a shared story, you can handle *anything*. It takes some time to get to a shared story, and you need space to be able to create a shared story. But it makes everything possible.

You can deal with any conflict if you have a shared vision, a shared story.

If you have two different stories, then you ultimately can't create lasting intimacy, and you can't create coherence—but it's the same thing all the way up and all the way down, at every scale. Whether that's within a family, an organization, within a company, at school—you need a shared story. **Shared story generates coherence and intimacy.**

So if we want to heal the global intimacy disorder, we need to create a shared story, and it has to be a shared story that's *real*. A shared story is based on one thing: shared value. There's no shared story without shared value. Let's review the intimacy formula to get a full sense of how to respond to the global intimacy disorder.

We define intimacy as a shared identity in the context of otherness, meaning **we share an identity, but we're also individuated, Unique Selves.** But our shared identity is union or fusion.

So intimacy, according to our equation, equals shared identity in the context of (relative) otherness, times:

- Mutuality of *recognition*—we recognize each other.
- Mutuality of *pathos*—we feel each other.
- Mutuality of *value*—there's a shared Field of Value between us.
- Mutuality of *purpose*—we have shared purpose, a shared story.

In order to heal the global intimacy disorder, we need to restore intimacy by generating a shared story, but that story can't be made-up conjecture.

It has to integrate the best knowledge we have—the best traditional values, the best modern values, and the best postmodern values—into a larger Field of Value, which serves as the ground of our shared story.

To sum this section up, we have:

1. *Generator Function of Existential Risk 1: A dominant cultural success story based on rivalrous dynamics and win/lose metrics.*

2. *Generator Function of Existential Risk 2: Complicated (fragile) systems, rather than complex (anti-fragile) systems.*

3. *Root cause of both functions: A Global Intimacy Disorder.*

4. *A shared story is required to restore intimacy.*

5. *There can be no shared story without a sense of shared value.*

6. *Intimacy = shared identity in the context of (relative) otherness x mutuality of recognition x mutuality of pathos x mutuality of value x mutuality of purpose*

5.4

SUMMARY OF THE GLOBAL INTIMACY DISORDER AS THE ROOT CAUSE OF EXISTENTIAL RISK, AND THE SIX REASONS WHY WE NEED A NEW STORY

If all this is true, it's very exciting because we're then in the place where we can heal the source code of culture. None of this is conceptual or theoretical. This is about **addressing the great suffering that's already with us, and potentially soon upon us in a much greater way, as we saw in Chapter One**. We know that we have to make this da Vinci move and facilitate a set of structures that can penetrate the source code and raise all boats.

The da Vinci move into modernity—at that time between worlds, at that time between stories—occurred before exponential tech created existential risk. None of that existed then.

The stakes are now of an entirely different nature— we're literally poised between utopia and dystopia.

In order to respond to existential and catastrophic risk, **we need a New Story based on a shared Field of Value**, what we've called *First Principles and First Values*. Let's go through the seven levels explaining why this is the case.

LEVEL ONE: EVERY SINGLE PROBLEM WE HAVE IS GLOBAL

Every potential existential risk we face is global. Therefore, local, circumscribed languages of value—which is what we had until now, governed by particular social conventions and by local religion—cannot help us in this situation.

This is why we initially started something called the Center for World Spirituality, with Ken Wilber—so we could talk about the undergirding values generally shared by all the traditions. We need a world spirituality because all our problems are global. **It's utter absurdity to address the global challenges of existential risk with local spiritualities.** We later decided that spirituality was too narrow a game, so we now have the Center for World Philosophy and Religion.

And since all our challenges are global, we need a global story.

We need a global ethos for a global civilization that emerges from a global story.

If we don't have a global story, we can't address the issues. Every issue we face requires global coordination. We need to coordinate, so we need to look at the issues and sense-make based on shared values. We can't create global coordination that will generate global coherence—for example, in response to Covid, which has been an utter disaster, unnecessarily killing millions—because we don't have shared sense-making. **We have a deeply broken global information ecology. This is how false certainties emerge.**

It's currently, virtually impossible to have shared sense-making at all. The amount of information people sent me about Covid that was based on unbelievably bad sense-making, on all sides of the issue, was utterly shocking—and that's just one issue of many.

We have a completely broken sense-making apparatus, and if we don't fix it, we can't have a shared sense of coordination. Unless we can create global coherence, we can't address even one of the ten huge existential risks we face. And crucially: **we can't do shared sense-making without a shared Ground of Value.** Values inform sense-making. Without value, you cannot do any shared sense-making whatsoever. You can't generate global coherence at a time when you have existential risk to the very future of humanity, which demands that coherence.

This is, in fact, an entrepreneurial movement, and we live in an entrepreneurial universe. We're all entrepreneurs—and in this context "entrepreneurship" means: *I'm going to take a risk, identify a need, and I'm going to create that which didn't exist before.* Entrepreneurs have gotten a bad name lately. They're seen as crazy, greedy, psychotic, self-involved. Some individuals are, for certain. But entrepreneurship is the movement of Reality, so let's do this together. We've got to be entrepreneurs of the future. We are indeed the *Office for the Future.*[12]

LEVEL TWO: WE NEED A NEW SHARED STORY OF VALUE, ROOTED IN SHARED EROS

What happens when there's no true Eros in play? We're left with pseudo-eros. The Universe never tolerates an erotic vacuum: there's either true Eros or pseudo-eros. If we're filled with Eros, we don't need pseudo-eros, but if we're in the emptiness, it's too painful and it rips us apart. If we don't have a shared Eros of Value, pseudo-eros comes creeping in to fill the void. It's the basis for the Success 2.0 story, rivalrous conflict based on win/lose metrics.

---

[12] Visit officeforthefuture.com.

Dunkirk is a fantastic film that shows all of Great Britain rallying and sending boats across the channel to liberate Europe. That's not pseudo-eros—that's Eros where there's a deeply shared value. The win/lose metrics disappear. There's a larger value at play. In the current context:

We're facing the death of humanity, but it must not make us insane. Instead, it must energize us with new joy, with new possibility, with new Eros.

We get to come together at this pivot point in history, between utopia and dystopia, and generate this new Eros of Value. If there's no Eros of Value grounded in a New Story based on First Principals and First Values then in its place you're guaranteed to have pseudo-eros of various forms.

LEVEL THREE: WE'RE RESPONSIBLE FOR THE PAST, PRESENT, AND FUTURE

The idea that we have a *responsibility* for the future doesn't live in us naturally, but it is a First Principle and First Value. There is a value that says, *I have a commitment to the future*. The covenant between generations is a deep, core value.

The total set of temporal First Principles and First Values is:

- I have a relationship and responsibility to the past—to my parents, to my grandparents, to my ancestors.
- I have a relationship and responsibility to the present—to what's in front of me right now.
- I have relationship and responsibility to the future—to the many who will come after me.

Past, present, and future are not mere details, but verifiable First Principles and First Values of Reality. Only if I can understand and transmit that, do

I understand that I have a responsibility to the future. It's why so many people don't pick up on this because unless I access that value and practice that value, I can't find it. The intergenerational relationship, the covenant between the generations—*the commitment to the future itself*—is a First Principle and First Value.

LEVEL FOUR: WE MUST RESPOND TO THE POTENTIAL DEATH OF OUR HUMANITY

We're not just threatened with the death of the entire human species, but there's an equally if not more dire dystopian scenario, which we've talked about in great length when describing the emerging technocracy we call TechnoFeudalism: the death of *our* humanity.[13]

What does it mean to think that I'm "freely choosing" something—what to think, who to vote for—when I'm being manipulated by the best machine intelligence in the world, which is exponentially smarter and more advanced than the one that defeated Boris Kasparov, the former world chess master? You've got that entire array of machine intelligence surveilling everything about you, knowing all your vulnerabilities and weaknesses, and doing split tests to evoke particular choices and behaviors. It's incredible—and quite terrifying.

We're in this world where we think we're choosing, but our real ability to choose is slowly disappearing, if it hasn't already. We'll soon be surrounded by biometric sensors where all our responses and feelings will be tracked and fed into machine intelligence. And it won't be a choice: we won't be able to get healthcare or insurance without a biometric sensor. Such a world, a world that's rapidly emerging, signals the death of our humanity—and we're tracking this very carefully, it's a key concern at the Center.[14] **Now, you can't challenge the death of our humanity unless you have First**

---

[13] See the forthcoming book: David J. Temple, *How Humanity Escapes the Global Skinner Box: Artificial Intelligence, TechnoFeudalism, and the Collapse of Value in the Digital Age.*

[14] To learn more about the *Center for World Philosophy and Religion*, see worldphilosohyandreligion.org.

Principles and First Values because, otherwise, *you don't know what our* *humanity is.*

For example, Google offers you a free email account. They made six declarations in 2003, including their right to all of the personal data of their end-users, even without asking them. So when Google offers us a free email account, they're also saying, "I have permission to read your Gmail, feed it into machine intelligence, create a personality profile based on your personhood, and sell the predictive analysis about how you're going to react to third parties in auctions that are taking place all the time—billions of auctions per second."

They decided they had that right because Google is founded by a couple of lovely postmodern guys who have no sense of the First Value of person-hood. **In our culture, a notion that there's a First Value of personhood simply does not exist.** It's been completely obliterated by a cyber-total-ism that dominates the tech plex—a (false) belief that animates everything that's going on today.

But if you don't have a clear sense of the fundamental and intrinsic First Value of personhood, *how are you going to challenge that?* You have no way to challenge it. All you have is Google saying it's not against the law. When there's no ground of Value, no Field of Value, you only have the law, and when the tech world is moving into worlds that never existed before, you're not actually going to have law anymore because *law only governs precedent.* It governs what happened before, but the nature of the tech world is that it's consistently moving into unprecedented territory, which means there can never be a truly just law. And a sense of inherent value is needed to ground law.

Google co-founders Sergey Brin and Larry Page, and most of the culture in fact, are naturally living without First Values. They would have to feel like they're living in a shared story, and that they're responsible to that shared story. They don't live in it now because the assumption is—like the assump-tion of Nadav Eyal and others—that there simply are no intrinsic values.

LEVEL FIVE: WE'RE ONLY INSPIRED TO ACTION BY VALUE

Why do you need First Principles and First Values? Because only value inspires us to act. It could be the value of Beauty—for example, *I need to be by the ocean, where I'm moved by the value of Beauty, so I'm going to do anything I can to get to that ocean.* We're inspired by Goodness, Truth, Beauty, and creativity, but **I'm only truly inspired—I'm only *truly moved* by them to act—when I recognize that their value is inherent.** Otherwise, their expression becomes founded in pseudo-eros.

We're inspired to align with value—and we're inspired to fight when a value has been violated.

We've already talked about how Black Lives Matter exploded because there was a terrible violation of value. George Floyd was murdered and we kept seeing that video play again and again. Everyone's worried about dying from a pandemic, and suddenly no one cares about that: *everyone* floods the streets—all over the United States and all over the world—because we all clearly saw a value being violated.

Even when we don't have a sense of a shared ground of value, it was so horrific that it pushed through our jaded consciousness. We viscerally felt the violation, we rose up and went into the streets—outraged, astonished, and motivated to defend that value.

But if you have no story that we transmit to our children and to our world—based on First Principles and First Values—you can never arouse others, and you can never activate political action or will.

Political will, social will, personal will is only activated in response to value.

The second you say there's no intrinsic value, the whole system begins to collapse.

We just sit glued to our Facebook feeds, going up and going down in our win/lose metrics, looking for a little pseudo-eros on the side—as the tech plex grows larger and larger. We upgrade our algorithms and downgrade humanity—what it means to be a human being—until, within a very short period of time, we may not recognize our very humanity.

So our response to the Global Intimacy Disorder must be a response grounded in the articulation of a New Story based on a new set of First Principles and First Values. That was the story of modernity, which emerged out of Florence. We need to do that again.

LEVEL SIX: VALUE CREATES ALLUREMENT AND INTIMACY

Again, the difference between a complicated and a complex system is that in a complex system, there's allurement between the parts, while there's no allurement in a complicated system. So here's the key question: *What creates allurement?* Value creates allurement.

In other words, when there's a shared ground of value—which is the ground of our shared story—we're allured, connected, intimate, part of the Intimate Universe. But we don't fuse together—it's a Unique Self Symphony of distinct and differentiated parts within the whole. There's enormous diversity that's real and beautiful, even though we're playing the same music. We're unique but connected, part of the same movement of Cosmos.

When we share value in this way, we're allured to each other. For example, two people may come from the same part of the country, with a similar dialect and with similar family structures. That itself creates a kind of allure-

236

ment—but that's still superficial, pseudo-erotic allurement. It's compelling, interesting, and arguably even important, but that's not real allurement. It's not really going to hold me, and it's certainly not what's going to hold all of us together.

Real allurement means: a shared ground of real, inherent value that's creative. That's what transforms a complicated system into a complex one, thereby mitigating existential risks due to fragility—complicated, fragile systems that break down become complex ones driven by allurement. And allurement means: *I feel you and you feel me.* I feel beyond my quarterly report, beyond my win/lose metrics, and I become "omni-considerate" for the sake of the whole:

- I consider the whole.
- I can feel into the whole.
- I'm allured to the whole.

Allurement between the parts itself is generated by fundamental value.

LEVEL SEVEN: INTIMACY CREATES OBLIGATION

The obligation to *genuine responsibility*—not obligation imposed by the old church or by the social structures of society—comes from a shared identity, a sense of deep intimacy with Reality. In the original Hebrew, the word for "obligation" and "love" are the same. Obligation is based on intimacy, connection, touch, Eros, love. **The more *intimate* we are, the more *committed* we are to each other.** *Intimacy creates obligation.* Isn't that beautiful?

It's one of the reasons that one of the hard positions I hold is that I'm against casual sex. I happen to believe that casual sex has no place in the world—because sex is intimate, and intimacy *always* creates obligation. There's nothing casual about it. A "casual" sexual encounter where you're never going to see the person again—no. *That's too much intimacy, and not enough responsibility.* Now, responsibility doesn't have to mean getting married, but it has to mean that there's total respect, that you hold the encounter in the sacredness of memory.

The more intimacy, the more obligation—that's gorgeous. This is not obligation that we feel bad about, but obligation that comes directly from our freedom. It's the free, gorgeous *choosing* of responsibility, **it's the joy of responsibility.**

The deeper my intimacy, the deeper my obligation—only if I recognize that intimacy is not a psychological construct, but a value.

Because if intimacy's just some casual, psychological construct, then who really cares about it? **Honor and nobility are created from intimacy because we recognize that intimacy is a fundamental First Value of Reality, part of the infrastructure of Cosmos itself.**

•　•　•

How do you create a New Story based on shared principles and values if the assumption—in the academy and media, and by people writing books like *Sapiens* and *Revolt*—is that there are no intrinsic values?

In other words: if the basic, mainstream intellectual understanding—which people are just taking as a given—is that there are no intrinsic values, then how do you create a shared story based on First Principles and First Values? It's a non-starter. It's a big problem, which everyone assumes cannot be solved:

- Religious people say that there's value that only comes from God.
- Modern secular people say that there are no intrinsic values; humans just make them up.

So we're stuck in polarization. Within the religions, everybody fights about whose values are right. Within the secular community—since we're making up our values—our values merely become part of our identities, so we fight about who's right. **We've got a completely polarized world at a moment where we most need coordination and coherence and intimacy.**

That's a summary of the global intimacy disorder at the root of existential risk, and the seven reasons why we desperately need a New Story.

5.5

VALUES IN PREMODERNITY, MODERNITY, AND POSTMODERNITY: ENGAGING WITH NATURAL LAW AND THE PERENNIAL PHILOSOPHY

In the traditional pre-modern period, everybody believed in value, and everybody believed that value could only come from God. Many felt that their job was to bring everybody else into *their* system of value, and if they didn't come willingly, the most valuable thing was to either convert them or kill them.

Now, at the same time, many of the premodern traditional systems—in their inner core—are expressions of very deep and true structures of value. But over time, those structures became confused, and it became difficult to distinguish between:

- Deep gnosis of the Good, the True, and the Beautiful—what we're going to call *depth structures of value*, and

- Rituals and customs local to a specific group of people with one system of exclusive belief—what we're going to call *surface structures of value.*

It was about *these* people, our people being triumphant over *those* people, or *this* religion being triumphant over *that* religion. The big win/lose competition of the traditional period is rivalrous conflict between the religions. Everybody agrees on value in the premodern period, and value is said to come from God, or to come from reason—but reason is said to be an instrument of God.

THE MODERN RESPONSE

Then along comes modernity, which has two big camps. The first, led by David Hume—and there's a straight line from Hume to postmodernity—who says: *at the very core of things, there's no intrinsic value*:

- God is not a source of value.
- Human beings create value.
- Value is not intrinsic to Cosmos in any way.

The second camp says: We're going to pick up on this earlier idea from premodernity—*there is in fact intrinsic value in Cosmos*—developing, refining it, and giving it a new name: "natural law." There is intrinsic value and it's the natural law of Cosmos. This comes from a lot of places, but it's very strong in Aquinas, then later in Smith, Comenius, and others. **Natural Law is the intrinsic, natural value that lives in the world, that tells us how to be and how to live.** Indeed, there's a whole school of modernist thinkers who said we have to adopt some version of natural law in response of the skeptical erosion of value.

There's another, related group of moderns who believe in intrinsic value, and they attempted to abstract from all religions the shared underlying truths, collecting them into what they call the "perennial philosophy"—meaning that which lasts throughout the ages.

So in modernity, you've got two schools:

- Those who say there is no intrinsic value, that humans completely create it.
- Those who say there is inherent, intrinsic value, founded not in God *per se*, but either in natural law or the perennial philosophy.

THE POSTMODERN RESPONSE

Modernity lasted from the Renaissance until about fifty years ago, and postmodernity really gets going after World War Two, it goes into major flowering in the 1990s. In one sense, postmodernity is modernity on steroids—Habermas' "hyper-modernity"—because it picks up this strain in modernity that says there can be no real value in the world.

As I've mentioned many times, Yuval Harari—who is not a philosopher, but a historian—represents the postmodern narrative that he has absorbed from his culture. There's no basis for value, he claims. For example, he writes that there's no difference between an Englishman going to liberate Jerusalem during the Crusades, massacring people along the way, and an Englishman going to the Promised Land 700 years later to work with refugees to help them get resettled. Both these men—one from the twelfth century, the other from the twenty-first—are living fictions. **For Harari, there's no intrinsic difference between the massacres done by one and the resettling of refugees done by the other. They're both social constructions of Reality, both figments of our imagination.**

To be fair, Yuval has done a good job of addressing some of the problems in the world. He himself understands that there's a great need for a New Story. But, like Nadav Eyal, he says explicitly: *There is no basis of a New Story and values. All stories are fictions.*

The other example Harari gives, in Chapter Two of *Sapiens*—is that he says there's no difference between a regime like Gaddafi's Libya, which destroys human rights, and our notion of universal human rights—they're both pure fictions. But he's just expressing the dominant culture, widely transmitted through the academy and the media. No one's even shocked by it—and that's a very big deal.

In postmodernity, we've completely deconstructed value, including both modern attempts to salvage it. The postmodern academy says that natural law and perennial philosophy don't work.

These were two modern attempts to create a Universal Grammar of Value, but those attempts have been decimated by the academy, and not entirely wrongly. For starters, perennial philosophy and natural law cannot be correct because they seem to ignore evolution, claiming that *there are only preordained and eternal values.*

For example, Howard Bloom points this out in his book, *The Lucifer Principle.* He used to be a dyed-in-the-wool postmodernist, and I believe he's shifting somewhat. But regarding the changing nature of Value, he looks, for example, at the idea of love. He says you can't call love an eternal value because 2,000 years ago, love meant that, if your wife disobeyed you, it was your *obligation* to beat her. Today, your wife should call the police if that happens—love today means something completely different.

Therefore, you can't call love some "natural law" value, because it means something completely different in various contexts. For example, Aquinas says that sex creates children according to natural law. Therefore, sex that is not for the sake of creating children is against the law. Well, that doesn't seem exactly right, as sex obviously has a much broader structure.

If Aquinas uses natural law to justify his ideas because that's what happens in nature, **it's very clear that whatever love means in the human world, it means something very much different in the animal world.** As we pointed out yesterday, if a lion is hungry and goes to eat a gazelle, the lion doesn't get arrested, but if I'm hungry and eat my friend Terry Nelson for breakfast, I'm definitely going to be arrested.

The notion that natural law is the same all throughout the world doesn't make sense.

Do you begin to see the problem? There are many other quite valid objections to both natural law and perennial philosophy, but the assumption is that those objections to these two modern expressions have completely knocked any hope for a return of intrinsic value out of the ballpark.

5.6

THE ETERNAL TAO
IS THE EVOLVING TAO:
THE INTIMACY OF EROS

Ijust summarized an enormous conversation to give you some sense of it. These critiques of natural law and the perennial philosophy are important and true in some sense, but very partial. Let's try to get a deeper sense of this and see how CosmoErotic Humanism responds to these valid critiques on natural law and perennial philosophy, and takes it the next step. We've already talked about the Tao, by which we mean the Field of Value—and we say that **the eternal Tao is the evolving Tao.**

This means that love, or Eros, is a principle of Cosmos. But love is not static—it evolves. Evolution itself—meaning the transformation to higher and deeper levels of exterior and interior structure—is a First Principle and First Value of Cosmos itself. Evolution is not an accident. Evolution is a structure of Cosmos.

So, for example, Eros as a First Value is an inherent and *evolving* structure of Reality, which looks different at each level:

- In the world of matter, from subatomic particles to planets and galaxies.

- In the world of life, from microorganisms, plants, and animals to ecosystems.
- In the world of humans, both individual and collective.

Eros, or love, will look different at every level of consciousness in the world of the human being, but there's also a shared force called Eros that moves through the whole thing, at all levels. That force is always the same, but it's also an evolving force—not merely a preordained, eternal, and unchanging value. Remember: **Eternity is not everlasting time, but points to what's beneath and beyond time.**

It's the time-less moment—that's eternity.

So the eternal Tao is the evolving Tao. Eros is a structure of Cosmos—and *Eros means the experience of radical aliveness desiring, seeking ever deeper contact and ever greater wholeness.*

Eros is the allurement between separate parts as they come together to create new wholes, which have more value than the sum of the individual parts. That structure exists everywhere, even between subatomic particles. Whitehead talks about the "appetition," the appetite, the desire of Cosmos. **Cosmos is filled with Eros, and that Eros lives between subatomic particles, which create new intimacies.**

Again, intimacy equals shared identity in the context of (relative) otherness, times mutuality of recognition, mutuality of pathos, mutuality of value, and mutuality of purpose. **That describes subatomic particles and galaxies, just as it exactly describes a human couple.**

Now we begin to see how Cosmos operates at all levels. There's an entire movement of Eros in the plant world. It exists in the world of fish. In the world of animals, there's an erotic interplay of allurement and what we would call love. Of course, it looks much different there than it does in the world of matter or humans or planets.

As a matter of fact, at each of these levels, it might have a much different name. In the world of matter, we might call allurement electro-magnetism, or the calibrated balance between attraction and repulsion. At a more cosmic level we may call it gravity. In other words, Eros animates the four fields, the four forces: the strong and the weak nuclear forces, electromagnetism, and gravity. Eros animates all these fields, moving Reality from quarks to culture, from mud to Mozart, from bacteria to Bach, from slime to Shakespeare…

When we get into the human world, the most complex form of organization, Eros—or what we call "love"—breaks out in a new way. In essence:

Love is Eros at the human level.

In addition, at every level of the human world, Eros breaks out in different ways:

- In **egocentric love**: I love myself and my family.
- With **ethnocentric love**, I love my whole tribe, and I'll even die for my tribe.
- Then, there's **worldcentric love**, which means I have a shared identity with every human being. We feel each other. If you're starving in Africa, I feel you. If you're in joy, I feel you. We have mutuality of value and mutuality of purpose. We are intimate.
- When we get to **cosmocentric love**, we feel the animals. We feel the plants. We feel the planet itself. That's a new Reality, just like subatomic particles come together to create a new shared identity called an atom.

All of a sudden, we have a value called Eros—or love—that lives at the level of matter, that lives at the level of life, that lives at the level of mind.

- It's an intrinsic value of Cosmos.
- It's an expression of the Tao.
- It's an expression of the Field of Value.

The emergence of *Homo amor*—the New Human and the New Humanity based on the New Story—is the deepest expression yet of Eros and intimacy.

5.7

VALUE LIVES IN US: THE "ANTHRO-ONTOLOGICAL" METHOD

How do we access the First Values and First Principles that will animate the New Story of humanity? **We don't locate them in nature—we instead look inside ourselves.** That's the big difference between CosmoErotic Humanism and natural law. It's what we call the "Anthro-Ontological Method": we're looking deep within our own interiors.

The mysteries are within us: every gluon, and every muon, every lepton, every hadron, and the entire subatomic, molecular, macromolecular, cellular, multicellular—indeed, all of Reality, all of matter and life—lives within us.

The entire Universe lives in us: the feeling, tone, and the gnosis of Reality lives in us. When I go inside and clarify my own interior, I get a sense of ontology, of what's real. When I go inside, into myself, I find value in myself. I can locate value. Nature's not necessarily going to tell me what's valuable.

When we see cats killing each other, then nature's not necessarily a good source of value—this is one of the valid critiques of natural law.

Instead, we look anthro-ontologically, following these steps:

One, we locate a value that seems to be intrinsic.

Two, we see if it's only *my own* value, or do all my friends share it? Is it more widespread? If so, we move on to the next step.

Three, does it only show up among people in the current era, or does it exist historically across time—have all or most people experienced some version of this apparently intrinsic value?

Four, does that value exist in some form only in the human world, or is there an earlier expression of that value in the animal world? It might have different expressions between matter, life, and mind—there's both continuity and discontinuity:

- Matter rises and triumphs into life.
- Life includes all of matter, but adds something that wasn't in matter at all—a cell adds something that molecules absolutely did not have.
- Then we go through all the levels of life and become a human being, which has all of the animal level, but adds something new that wasn't there before.
- At every level of human consciousness, we add a new emergent.

That's what evolution means: through continuity and discontinuity, there's a new emergent at every level. There's a thread of love or a thread of Eros that moves from matter to life to mind, through every level of human consciousness.

Eros, love, appears in one way at the level of matter, another way at the level of life, and another way at the level of the human mind and culture.

• • •

As an example, let's take something like fairness or justice. Critics of natural law rightly ask: where could fairness possibly live in the world of matter? Obviously, there's no fairness in the world of matter, but what does fairness actually mean? **Fairness means right relationship between the parts, indicating that everything is where it needs to be—and a name for that at non-human scales could be *harmony*.**

So in the first nanoseconds of the Big Bang, one of the core structures of Reality is harmony, which is related to the human notion of fairness. That harmony is driven by allurements. The material world continues to develop because three quarks—in a particular configuration of allurement—form a right relationship between the parts. We would call that right relationship harmony and allurement in the world of matter, and it's going to have a different name in the world of life. Then when we get to the human world, that notion of harmony is going to erupt, in this conscious way, into what we call "fairness."

Our understanding of fairness itself is going to evolve further and further, but it's connected to more basic forms of harmony. What we just did is reconstruct our understanding of the Cosmos. **This is a way to know how intimacy operates all the way up and all the way down**—across economics, across governance, across organizations, across entrepreneurship, across attachment theory, across the various schools of psychology, across the various forms of physics and molecular biology.

All of a sudden, we realize we're at home in the Cosmos.

It's one Cosmos. It's one world. It's one love. It's one heart. It's one value.

The same principle of intimacy operates all the way up and all the way down, but there's a core value at the very heart of Cosmos—Eros—and then there are many dimensions of this.

If we get this right, it could change everything. We've got to research properly in every field and demonstrate that this New Story of the universe is

251

not just fanciful conjecture. **This is not merely New-Age speculation or fundamentalist dogma.** *It's the core structure of Reality.* **This is a story based on First Values and First Principles that operate all the way up and all the way down across the board.**

We're in the Tao, but the Tao is not, as Nadav Eyal has assumed, just traditional, preordained, and eternal values. He's just repeating what he's been told, that values must only be preordained and eternal. It's very easy to critique that simplistic idea.

In fact, the eternal Tao is the *evolving* Tao. Once you see this, it changes everything. **Eros is an eternal First Principle and First Value—and Eros also evolves.**

We call that the evolution of love.

Let's sit with this for a moment in Silence of Presence.

5.8

FIRST PRINCIPLES IN *BLACK WIDOW*: THE VALUE OF FAMILY

W̲e're going to take a look at a "sacred text of culture" that beautifully demonstrates all of this: the Marvel movie *Black Widow*. We're going to go through a bunch of scenes from the entire movie, just to get a deep look at how First Principles and First Values are everywhere. I'll offer short interpretations after each scene, and we'll be looking at one value in particular, just to get a sense of how all values generally operate.

[Note: These scenes were played at the 2021 Eros Mystery School. The extensive scenes and dialogue included below are intended to give a sense of the transformative power of value.]

MOVIE CLIPS: *BLACK WIDOW*

1—OPENING SCENE, SETTING THE CONTEXT

[In the opening scene of the film, it's a sunny day in a typical ideal American suburb in Ohio. Children are playing outside, riding their bikes. Two girls (Yelena and Natasha) are running around in the backyard, when Yelena falls and is comforted by her mother

(Melina). At one point she says to her daughter, "Your pain only makes you stronger." Once it starts to get dark, they are mesmerized by some fireflies, as Melina givers her children science lessons on bioluminescence. Then at the dinner table, it's a typical American family scene, as the father (Alexei) returns home after a day at work. Something is up, however, as Alexei seems troubled. The parents speak privately in another room.]

Melina: How long do we have?

Alexei: I don't know. Like, an hour, maybe.

Melina: I don't wanna go.

Alexei: Don't say that.

[Back at the dinner table, Alexei makes an announcement.]

Alexei: Girls… you remember when I told you that one day we'd have that big adventure? Well, today's the day.

Yelena: Yay!

Melina (to Natasha): I'm sorry.

[Alexei is quickly but calmly packing a rifle and other weapons, while chatting with his kids, telling them they must pack and leave very soon. Natasha goes to pick up the photo album, but Melina, the mother, tells her to leave it there. Alexei then pulls out a computer disk and shows Melina. In the car, they speed off as the children look out the window at their neighborhood, presumably for the last time.]

Yelena: Where are we going?

Melina: Home.

Yelena: Mommy, you're silly. We just left home.

[They drive past police checkpoints that are just starting to block off the neighborhood, as Alexei puts a tape cassette in the deck, and "American Pie" starts to play, and they all sing along.

They drive down a backroad, and enter what looks to be a military base. Alexei grabs the rifle, while Natasha grabs a picture of her and her sister before leaving the car. Mother and kids pile into a small plane. Police officers arrive and Alexei shoots at them, while Melina starts accelerating the plane for lift-off.

Alexei jumps on the wing of the plane, as police officers are firing at the plane, wounding Melina. While Alexei is still shooting at the police, the plane dramatically lifts off just in time and they're airborne.]

So far we've got a family—two sisters, mom, dad. They're singing "American Pie." Then something happens, and they've got to make this dramatic escape. They end up landing in Cuba, where we realize something's wrong—they weren't exactly a family. They were working for this guy named Dreykov, one of the heads of the Russian KGB, this villainous, evil figure. They were stealing something. He gives them a computer disc. We start to wonder about the two girls, and it becomes pretty apparent that they're not the couple's real daughters, and we're about to see that the girls are going to be separated. They're each going to be trained to become "widows," meaning trained assassins, for Dreykov. The whole scene we saw in Ohio was the parents involved in deep undercover spy work.

2—"MY GIRLS ARE THE TOUGHEST"

[On a military base, the two girls see their "father" Alexei, and Yelena yells "Daddy," but he doesn't respond. She starts running towards him, as officers grab her. Natasha yells, kicks a soldier and grabs his gun, pointing it at the soldiers and threatening to shoot.]

Natasha: Don't touch her! I will kill you all! *[Speaking Russian]* I will shoot. Don't touch her.

Alexei: Honey. You're gonna need to hand me that gun.

Natasha: I don't wanna go back there. I wanna stay in Ohio. You can't take her... you can't. She's only six.

Alexei: You were even younger. It's okay. Come here. Do you know why it's gonna be all right? 'Cause my girls are the toughest girls in the world. You're gonna take care of each other, okay? Everything's gonna be fine.

Here we see that the older daughter, Natasha, has already been trained as a fighter. She grabs the gun, starts talking in Russian, threatens the soldiers. We don't quite yet know that they're not the daughters, but we begin to understand something else is happening here. She says her sister Yelena is "too young"—meaning too young to be trained to become an assassin. The "father," Alexei, says it's going to be okay... "because my girls are the toughest girls in the world." We start with this family scene. Then we realize the scene is not what it looked like at all. We realize that dad and mom and the family are not real—they're working for Dreykov.

There's this moment where Yelena, the younger daughter, says, "Daddy," and he doesn't respond. As the credits roll, we see all these scenes of Dreykov, as one of the most powerful human beings in the world, with different heads of state, with President Clinton and all sorts of people. He's clearly depicted as someone pulling the strings behind the scenes, running this covert structure of the world from a perspective of evil. The daughters are in his Black Widow organization.

3—A FAMILY TORN APART

[As the credits of the movie are displayed, we see different scenes of young girls being captured, scenes of them as normal girls, screaming

256

as they're separated from their siblings, as Dreykov is watching his soldiers carry out his orders, such as: "Remove all the defects."

Natasha and Yelena are forcefully separated as they're screaming. Before they're separated, Natasha manages to secretly pass something to Yelena. Afterwards, Dreykov bends down and takes Natasha's face in his hands, and says, "The Red Room is your home now," as she yells and fights back.]

Here we see Dreykov, who's essentially captured these girls and enlisted them in his Black Widow assassin team. Natasha doesn't see Yelena again for a long time, and in the next scene, we fast-forward twenty years. Natasha grows up to be one of the most talented assassins for Dreykov, so she's targeted by a super-hero team called the Avengers, who capture her and invite her to defect. Of course, she's been wanting to defect her whole life, and she becomes part of the Avengers family. It's a long story, but now she's somewhat estranged from them, and so we pick up from there.

4—"I HAVE FRIENDS"

[Natasha approaches a trailer in the woods, drawing a weapon, suspecting someone is in there. She enters the trailer, and then the bedroom, where she sees someone sleeping on the bed: it's Rick Mason, an agent she hired to get her some new passports.]

Natasha: Did you get everything on my list?

Rick Mason: Got passports, entry visas, a couple of local driver's licenses. Mix and match, you should be able to stretch it to twenty or so identities. Hey, are you okay?

Natasha: Why wouldn't I be?

Rick Mason: I hear things. You know, something about the Avengers getting divorced… You can tell me, you know. That's the way the whole "friends" thing works.

Natasha: I know. I have friends.

Rick Mason: People who have friends don't call me.

Natasha: And I don't pay you to worry.

Oh, hey. What's all this junk?

Rick Mason: Oh, just some mail and personals from the Budapest safe house.

In that box from Budapest is a vial of this chemical agent able to de-program widows. It works in a second, and they're awoken from the trance that Dreykov has put them in—he's essentially robbed them of free will and is exercising a kind of mind control. Along with this chemical, there's the picture of her and Yelena. She realizes that her sister must have sent her these chemical vials. She hasn't seen her sister since that earlier scene, twenty years ago. She then realizes her sister must be somehow involved in something and she goes to Budapest to find her.

5—"YOU'VE GROWN UP"

[Her gun drawn, Natasha enters the Budapest safehouse. Yelena hears her and calls out from the other room.]

Yelena: I know you're out there.

Natasha: I know you know I'm out here.

Yelena: Then why are you skulking about like it's a minefield?

Natasha: Because I don't know if I can trust you.

Yelena: Funny, I was going to say the same thing.

Natasha: So, we gonna talk like grown-ups?

Yelena: Is that what we are?

[Fight scene between the two sisters, both highly trained assassins, which ends in a sort of mutual strangle hold, so they declare a truce.]

The sisters Yelena and Natasha are reunited and they're all grown up. They realize that Dreykov is still alive, although Natasha thought she had killed him before she left to become part of the Avengers. Yelena also had left the widows and she received, through a secret network, these chemicals that can deprogram people. Natasha invites Yelena to join her to take down Dreykov—but is she actually her sister? We realize she may not really be her "sister," as they discuss what happened in the last twenty years. Watch the dialogue, as **the key value of family becomes more clarified, as the depth and value of their relationship is questioned—a proxy for the culture at large.**

6—"NOT MY REAL SISTER"

[After their fight, the two sisters are talking in the kitchen.]

Natasha: I thought that you got out and were living a normal life.

Yelena: And you just never made contact again?

Natasha: Honestly, I thought you didn't wanna see me.

Yelena: Bullshit. You just didn't want your baby sister to tag along, whilst you saved the world with the cool kids.

Natasha: You weren't really my sister.

Yelena: And the Avengers aren't really your family.

When Natasha says, "You weren't really my sister" the dejected look on Yelena's face says it all. Then she defensively says: "And the Avengers weren't really your family." There's family confusion here, which is also a deeper confusion of values, as we'll see. Natasha and Yelena then decide that they're going to go find Alexei, their "father" in their pretend family. Because he was a close associate of Dreykov, they'll force Alexei to lead them to Dreykov to take down his "Red Room," where he's essentially been enslaving the girls he trains as assassins. First they need to break Alexei out of prison, in a big action scene, and they get him on a helicopter. In this next scene, they're together again, after all these years.

7—A "FAMILY" REUNITED

[The sisters are in the front seats of the helicopter, while Alexei, now rescued, is in the back, shouting down to his former captors. Then he joins his former daughters up front.]

Alexei: Oh, that was exciting. I'm so proud of you girls...

[Yelena turns and punches Alexei hard in the face.]

Alexei: [Groans] Okay, why the aggression, huh? Is it your time of the month?

Yelena: I don't get my period, dipshit. I don't have a uterus.

Natasha: Or ovaries.

Yelena: Yeah. That's what happens when the Red Room gives you an involuntary hysterectomy. They kind of just go in and they rip out all of your reproductive organs. They just get right in there and they chop them all away. Everything out, so you can't have babies.

Alexei: Okay, okay! You don't have to get so clinical and nasty.

Yelena: Oh, well, I was about to talk about fallopian tubes, but okay.

Alexei: It means so much to me that you came back for me.

[The sisters are disgusted, openly angry about his display of affection. But the true value of family is starting to emerge here.]

Natasha: No. No. You're gonna tell us how to get to the Red Room.

Alexei: Little Natasha, all indoctrinated into the Western agenda.

Natasha: I chose to go west to become an Avenger because they treated me like family.

Alexei: Really? Family? Well, where are they now? Where is that family now?

Natasha: Tell me where the Red Room is.

[Alexei laughs and then launches into a story about how he was trained as Russian super soldier, recruited and then betrayed by Dreykov, who sent him to Ohio for many years, threw him in prison for apparently killing his daughter, which he clearly didn't. The two sisters soften a little bit as Alexei tells his story, but they're still not totally buying it. They're clearly still very wounded after what happened when they were kids—and understandably so. Then he tells them that Melina (their "mother") is still alive and working for the Red Room, so they decide to find her.]

• • •

This is a weird and fascinating scene. They've broken him out of prison. He says, "Girls, it means so much to me that you rescued me"—but of course they're not *actually* his daughters. Even Natasha says: "I went to the Avengers because they treated me like family," a clear reference to her childhood. We've got this strong family theme that's appearing. Then, Alexei says, "Well, where are they now, if they were your family?"

261

There's this strange moment. She went to the Avengers because they treated her like family, not like him—but we know that, of course, Alexei's not her *real* father. He's a Russian agent. They're all agents, in fact. On the other hand, if you watch carefully, Alexei says: He buried me in Ohio, in the middle of this terrible undercover scene, and I was so bored, and it was so horrible and terrible there. When he says that, you notice that Yelena looks back at him because he's describing those years when he was playing their parent. He's describing those years as complete horror, and she's devastated by that in some way. But why would that be the case if they weren't real family?

8—FATHERLY PRIDE

[In the next scene, they run out of gas, and make a dramatic landing in the wilderness. On the ground, outside of the helicopter, the three of them are arguing.]

Alexei: What is it with this tension? Did I do something wrong?

Yelena: Is that a serious question?

Alexei: I only ever loved you girls. I did my best to make sure you would succeed to achieve your fullest potential, and everything worked out.

Natasha: Everything worked out?

Alexei: Yes. For you, yes. We accomplished our mission in Ohio. Yelena, you went on to become the greatest child assassin the world has ever known. No one can match your efficiency, your ruthlessness. And Natasha—not just a spy, not just toppling regimes, destroying empires from within, but an Avenger. You both have killed so many people. Your ledgers must be dripping, just gushing red. I couldn't be more proud of you.

Look at the strange play here. They're not his daughters, but he's hugging and praising them like they are, telling them how proud he is. On the other hand, when they're on the plane and he describes his time in Ohio, he says it was the most boring, terrible thing in the world. There's this very strange relationship here. They're technically not biologically related, and yet the next scene complicates things, once they find Melina, and are all re-united as a "family" unit. It's a long scene, but a very important one.

9—THE FAMILY CONSTRUCT

[Alexei and the sisters have found Melina at her property, and she welcomes them into her house, where she offers them food and drink. They are appropriately suspicious of her.]

Melina: Welcome to my humble abode. Make yourself at home. Let's have a drink.

Natasha: Are there any booby traps around here? Anything we need to know about?

Melina: I didn't raise my girls to fall into traps.

Natasha: You didn't raise us at all.

Melina: Oh, maybe so. But if you got soft, it wasn't on my watch.

[Alexei is grunting as he's putting on his old Soviet super-soldier Red Guardian outfit, and then joins them at the table. Melina whistles and applauds, while the daughters are not impressed.]

Alexei: The family is back together again.

Melina: Seeing as our family construct was just a calculated ruse that only lasted three years, I don't think that we can use this term anymore, can we?

Natasha: Agreed. So, here's what's gonna happen…

Melina: Natasha, don't slouch.

Natasha: I'm not slouching.

Melina: Yes, yes, you are.

Natasha: I don't slouch.

Melina: You're going to get a back hunch.

Alexei: Listen to your mother.

Natasha: All right, enough. All of you.

Yelena: I didn't say anything. That's not fair.

Natasha: Here's what's gonna happen…

Yelena: I don't want any food.

Melina: Eat a little something, Yelena, for God's sake.

Natasha: You're gonna tell us the location of the Red Room. Finding Dreykov is not a fantasy. It's unfinished business.

Melina: You can't defeat a man who commands the very will of others. You never saw the culmination of what we started in America.

In this somewhat comedic scene, you can see the value of family again emerge. They're home, falling into old patterns, but of course they're not *really* home. There's some romantic and sexual tension between Melina and Alexei, but, more important is when Melina says: "I didn't raise my girls to fall into traps. You didn't get soft on my watch." Around the table, they act as the old family, but of course we can't say they're a family. It was all a staged cover-up, and yet she's still treating them like she's their mother. "Don't slouch. You'll be a hunchback." There's all these exchanges. Are they a family or not? They seem to be agreeing that the family thing's completely absurd and yet here they are, sitting around this table, like a family. Here the scene continues.

10—"THIS FAKE FAMILY WAS REAL TO ME"

[The door opens and a pig walks into the kitchen.]

Natasha: Did that pig just open the door?

Melina: Yes. It did. Good boy, Alexei.

[Melina has a tablet computer and she is adjusting some settings that have something to do with controlling the pig.]

Melina: Stop breathing.

[Pig Alexei grunts.]

Melina: We infiltrated the North Institute in Ohio. It was a front for S.H.I.E.L.D. scientists. Actually, it was Hydra scientists at that time. In conjunction with the Winter Soldier project, they had dissected and deconstructed the human brain to create the first and only cellular blueprint of the basal ganglia, the hub for cognition, voluntary motor movement, procedural learning. We didn't steal weaponry or technology. We stole the key to unlocking free will.

[Pig Alexei groans and falls over.]

Natasha: What are you doing?

Melina: Oh, I am explaining that the science is now so exact, the subject can be instructed to stop breathing and has no choice but to obey.

Natasha: Okay, you made your point. That's enough.

Melina: Well, don't worry, Alexei could've survived eleven more seconds without oxygen. Good boy. Now, you go back, back home where it's safe.

[Pig Alexei grunts, slowly gets up, and stumbles out of the kitchen.]

Melina: The world functions on a higher level when it is controlled. Dreykov has chemically subjugated agents planted around the globe.

Yelena: And do you know who they test it on?

Melina: Hmm… No. That's not my department.

Alexei: Ah, come on, come on. Don't lie to them. Hmm?

Natasha: Shut up! You are an idiot. And you're a coward. You're a coward. And our family was never real, so there's nothing to hold on to. We're moving on.

Alexei: Never family, huh? In my heart, I am simple man. And for a couple deep undercover Russian agents, I think we did pretty great as parents, huh? Yes, we had our orders, and we played our roles to perfection.

Natasha: Who cares? That wasn't real.

Yelena: Don't say that. Please don't say that. It was real. It was real to me. You are my mother. You were my real mother. The closest thing I ever had to one. The best part of my life was fake. And none of you told me.

"We were never a family, it was all fake," says Natasha. And then Yelena says: "Don't say it was fake. This is all I had." There's this realization that dawns. This is actually the pivot point of the movie. Melina, the mother, says: "We played our role to perfection," and Alexei says: "For a couple of deep undercover agents, I thought we did good." We think they weren't a family; we think it was a joke.

But all of a sudden, a strong value appears: family. Family is a value, and even though they were just *playing* family, nonetheless when you practice a value, the value has energy. The value itself is a strange attractor. *The value creates Reality because it is grounded in the Real.*

Dreykov is standing against another major human value: freedom, free will. He uses this group of undercover agents to steal that value, which signals the death of our humanity. That key sentence spoken by Melina—"a world that can be controlled operates at a higher level"—precisely echoes the sentiments of B.F. Skinner, the great psychologist and (hidden) mentor of Alex Pentland, current head of the MIT Media Lab, which greatly influences technology companies like Google and Facebook. **They're creating a system in which the world's totally controlled, in which freedom's undermined.** Bracket that for a second.

So Dreykov used this "family" to get access to the secrets of controlling free will, but what happened was that they end up playing out another value, family, even though they're play-acting. By living the value of family—with its connection, care, and intimacy—something happens and the value draws them in.

Now we're going to see two separate conversations that revolve around this family, first between mother and daughter, and then between father and daughter. Is the underlying value still there, and if so, does it still have power to guide decisions and behavior?

11—A HARD HEART SOFTENS

Natasha: I wish I could believe that you cared. But you're not even the first mother that abandoned me.

Melina: No, you weren't abandoned. You were selected by a program that assessed the genetic potential in infants.

Natasha: I was taken?

Melina: I believe a bargain was struck, your family was paid off. But your mother, she never stopped looking for you. She was like you in that way. She was relentless.

Natasha: I thought about her every day of my life. Whether or not I admitted it to myself, I did.

Melina: I've always found it best not to look into the past. Let's stop this. Do you know I was cycled through the Red Room four times before you were even born? Those walls are all I know. I was never given a choice.

Natasha: But you're not a mouse, Melina. You were just born in a cage, but that's not your fault.

Melina: Tell me, how did you keep your heart?

Natasha: Pain only makes us stronger. Didn't you tell us that? What you taught me kept me alive.

Melina: I'm sorry. I already alerted the Red Room. They'll be here any minute.

Melina says, "It's best not to think about the past." But she's kept this photo album with all the pictures from that time. Could the value of the family be real? Then Milena says: I had no choice. It's all about being a human and the value of free will. **There are two values at play here: family and freedom.** Natasha says: "You were born in a cage, but that's not who you are." Your humanity, the value of your humanity is still there. It's an incredible scene.

When you watch the face of Melina, the mother, in the last twenty minutes you see that she's been transformed. Although she's already alerted Dreykov, here she reclaims the value of family, and apologizes. Even though it's not biologically real, this value of family runs deeper. The same thing's going to happen to Alexei and Yelena in the next scene, and then, before Dreykov's people arrive, they're all going to make a plan. Value is going to bring the family back together, and that value is going to change everything.

12—"YOU KNOW, FATHERS"

Alexei: So, there I am ice fishing with my father. It's very cold day in this little ice shed. Cold even for Russia, you know? I'm reaching for a fish, and I lose balance. Ah! Splash! My hands go in the river. In this weather, frostbite sets in quick. My father, he go toilet on my hands.

Yelena: Oh, my God.

Alexei: Urine is 35 degrees Celsius, staves off the frostbite.

Yelena: How is this relevant?

Alexei: You know, fathers.

Yelena: No. You have done nothing but tell me how bored you were. I was the chore, the job you didn't want to do. To me, you were everything. But you don't care. You don't care. The only thing you care about are your stupid glory days as the Crimson Dynamo, and no one wants to hear about it. Get out!

[After a moment in silence, he starts sweetly singing "American Pie," Yelena's favorite childhood song, and she eventually joins in.]

As with the mother, the value of family draws the father in. He's finding that moment—this was her favorite song. This is the song they sang in the car in the opening scene. It's family. It's the picture of the two of them together that brings Natasha and Yelena together, and now it's her favorite song that creates the value of family.

Dreykov's people from the Red Room soon arrive and arrest all of them. We think they've all been captured, but we're going to realize that they've made a plan. In these scenes, **they were transformed by the value of family.** Even though they were play-acting, the value still had gravity. It's a strange attractor. The value has power, and it's going to challenge the tyrannical order of Dreykov—and succeed.

In the final action scenes of the movie, they end up relying on each other, trusting each other, connecting in a way that speaks of the true value of family. Amidst all the fighting and action, there are some scenes when the parents apologize to their children for their betrayal, and praise them for who they've become. Once, when Alexei and Melina have a chance to escape with their lives, they return to save their "daughters."

And in one poignant scene as Yelena and Natasha are falling through the air, Natasha turns to the younger one and says, in Russian, "Forgive me, my little sister. I should've come back for you." Yelena replies, "You don't have to say that. It's okay." And Natasha finally admits, "Hey, it was real for me, too." Remember what she said to her in the beginning: "You're not my sister. It wasn't real." Now, she says: "Forgive me, little sister. I should have come back. It was real."

That's the value.

That's the play of the Tao.

That's what takes down Dreykov—that's what confronts evil, or anti-value.

Value is what transforms Reality.

Value is a living being, a living energy. That's family—and families come back together. They all enact the value of family, even though they didn't intend to, even though they didn't initially subscribe to the value of family. In fact, Dreykov would find powerless girls who were *abandoned* by their families, or he would take them from their families, and he would say: *This is your new home.* Dreykov represents pseudo-family, the opposite of family. He's anti-family. He destroys them. He takes away the human value of freedom, of free will. Melina, the mother, thinks she's trapped in it. "I had no choice," she says. Her daughter Natasha says, "No, you did. You don't have to be a coward."

This is the draw and the pull of value. It's their reuniting as a family that allows them to take down Dreykov's entire organization—none of the pseudo-erotic surface structures in the world could challenge Dreykov. He reigned supreme. The only thing that undermined his tyranny was the value of family and the value itself transformed them.

They enacted the value of family for many years, even though it wasn't biologically real. And this speaks to something very important: **When you practice a real value, even if you don't fully subscribe to it—it can still *transform* you.** It brings them back together in this archetypal, mythical story. When the father, Alexei, sings "American Pie" with Yelena, and when Melina and Natasha see the old photo album, the value comes and completely transforms them.

Each of them makes powerful new choices.

That's the power of value.

5.9

THE EVOLUTIONARY HOMO AMOR FAMILY

So friends, where does our true power rest? We need more finances, yes. We need more human power. We need more editorial power. We need more research power. That's all absolutely true and real, but the core of our power is family—and we need to move beyond the old notion of family. Of course, the old notion of family's important and critical, so we include it.

My biological family is wonderful and critical. I'm madly committed to my biological family—and, to the best extent that we can, we should be. It's so gorgeous because, obviously, the intention of Cosmos was for us to get together. That's what biology means. Sometimes it's difficult and sometimes it's complex, and we *completely and totally* embrace all of that.

But there's a next level of family: my evolutionary family, my *Homo amor* family. Those are the people with whom I share a vision, the people with whom I share deep values. In the sixteenth-century interior sciences of the Hebrew wisdom tradition, that notion of family was called a "soul root family." Perhaps they didn't quite know what it meant then. Now, we know a bit more about what it means—evolution brought us together. Think about your evolutionary family. How do you even know each other? How unlikely is it that you were attracted together?

We are drawn together, allured by value.

The intimate movement, the Eros of Cosmos, brought us together and created, between us, a dimension of family and that's our power. The power of the *Homo amor* family is the power to transform tyranny. To stop a world which is about technocratic control through the effacing of free will. To invite value into the very heart of what it means to be a human being and to activate will. What activates the will of Alexei and Melina? Family. That's what challenges anti-value, that's what takes down Dreykov.

WE ARE *HOMO AMOR* FAMILY

Imagine that we expand our family from the ones we know—our egocentric family—to an ethnocentric vision. Now, we've got this larger family, the whole tribe. Then, we expand further to include every human being, quite literally, in our *Homo amor* family. Then we include every animal. We expand our intimacy more and more. **That's the evolution of love.**

That's the value of family—although it looks different in every age, and there are obviously corruptions of that value—but one of the structures of Reality is that there's a relationship among us. That relationship is real. That relationship means one thing among trees that are joined at the root level. It means particular things in the animal world. And it means different things in the human world—and then different things at every level of the human world—but it's a value that stands, and it's a value that expands.

This is the evolution of family, the embracing of *Homo amor* family, and that's what Avicii meant when he said: *Hey, brother. Hey, sister.*

Let's close with that prayer from Avicii. The invitation is: from our hearts to the hearts of everyone you know, and to everyone you don't—from my heart to your heart, your heart to my heart—connect with everyone that you can.

> ### PRAYER—"HEY BROTHER," AVICII
>
> *Hey brother*
> *There's an endless road to rediscover*
> *Hey sister*
> *Know that water's sweet, but blood is thicker*
> *Oh, if the sky comes falling down*
> *For you*
> *There's nothing in this world I wouldn't do*
>
> *Hey brother*
> *Do you still believe in one another?*
> *Hey sister*
> *Do you still believe in love? I wonder*
> *Oh, if the sky comes falling down*
> *For you*
> *There's nothing in this world I wouldn't do*
>
> *What if I'm far from home?*
> *Oh brother, I will hear you call*
> *What if I lose it all?*
> *Oh sister, I will help you out*
> *Oh, if the sky comes falling down*
> *For you*
> *There's nothing in this world I wouldn't do*

In this prayer, we are feeling our evolutionary family. And the value of family is absolutely real. It means something different than just biological family, as sacred as that is. It's a new structure. We have to work out the full

FIRST PRINCIPLES & FIRST VALUES

ramifications of what it means and how it works. We have full autonomy, we have different levels of how we express our commitment, but it's real. It wasn't biologically real in *Black Widow*—it was real because something happened in their being together.

Similarly, *Homo amor* family has to evolve to a new level. It's not too big and it's not too ambitious.

We can turn to each other and we can say: *Hey, brother. Hey, sister. There's nothing in this world I wouldn't do for you.*

Thank you so much.

INDEX